TOP NOTCH 2
TEACHER TIPS
SEASONS AND HOLIDAYS

**EDITED BY
ROSEMARY ALEXANDER**

SCHOLASTIC
PROFESSIONAL BOOKS

New York • Toronto • London • Auckland • Sydney

Designed by Intergraphics
Cover design by Vincent Ceci
Illustrations by David Blaisdell, Terri Chicko, Joe Chicko, Michelle Fridkin

ISBN 0-590-49122-9

Printed in the U.S.A.

Contents

Introduction

We all know that seasons and holidays are exciting events for children. And when that excitement is channeled into a math game or a creative poem, then learning is exciting too. But, all too often, a special day or event is upon us before we realize it and the teachable moment is lost. Or, when we do remember the day, we can't seem to think of an effective way to tie it into our curriculum.

Welcome to *Top-Notch Teacher Tips: Seasons and Holidays*. Within its pages are hundreds of ideas culled from *Instructor* magazine—all geared to a season, a special event, or a holiday. Spend a few moments right now to browse through it. Start with the first chapter, which will help you get ready for that all-important first day of school. Here are welcome-back bulletin boards, get-acquainted games, and lively orientation activities. Then glance at the September ideas, jotting down those that especially appeal to you. Does the first day of fall always slip by too quickly? Is Native American Day over before you know it? Not this year!

As each month approaches, look through its chapter and plan for those days you don't want to miss. You will find unique ways to use Halloween for math brush-ups, Thanksgiving for creative writing, and President's Day for historical research. You'll also discover an array of seasonal games, science experiments, social studies projects, reproducible activity pages, and more.

Top-Notch Teaching Tips: Seasons and Holidays is a resource you'll turn to again and again. Read it, enjoy it, and use its tips to enrich your class' learning experience all year long.

Start the School Year Right

Introduction

Being prepared is an important part of a successful first day. Start now to plan and create the things you'll need on that hectic first day of school.

Welcome to third grade. I'm so glad that you are in my class. We will study butterflies and whales, and find out how our town is run. Don't forget to bring a blank notebook. We'll all be keeping journals this year.

Welcome Letter

Start the year with a personalized letter welcoming students and their parents, like that illustrated here. Include in your message important class goals you want to reach. Add any special supplies kids need or a brief list of books to read to ensure smooth sailing this year!
JENELLE BERRY

Get-Acquainted Quiz

Here's a non-threatening quiz students can take to test what they know about their school. Before the first day, write up a list of questions to ask students, such as: What is the school address? Telephone number? How many students are in this school? How many students in your room? What is the principal's name? School secretary's? Librarian's? Custodian's?

When you're ready to give the quiz, write the answers in scrambled order on the chalkboard. Then read the questions aloud and ask kids to answer on paper, referring to the chalkboard as needed. Go over the questions and discuss what kids did and didn't know. What other questions do children have about the school? You'll encourage new or shy students to voice concerns without being self-conscious.
REBECCA WEBSTER GRAVES

First-Day Detectives

To familiarize students with the location of important items in the classroom, make them explorers. Give each student a list of items to locate, such as the pencil sharpener, light switch, drawing paper, scissors, crayons, dictionaries, wastepaper basket, and so on. Students should also locate special signs and any other objects that will be important to them throughout the year. As children find objects, they should cross them off their lists.
LUANN WILLIAMS

Start the School Year Right

Penny Welcome

On the first day of school, give each child a penny minted in the current year. Point out the differences among pennies — scratches, colors, brightness — and remind kids that, like the pennies, they're all equally valuable to you. Encourage children to save the penny as a token of your good wishes for the coming year.

KATHY O'BRIEN   BETH KREUTER

Welcome, New Class!

Many children feel uneasy entering a new classroom, especially those in the early grades. Start the year on a positive note with the following ideas to help your class feel secure and welcome.
- Display work done by your students from the previous year as a preview of things to come.
- Read your previous year's class list. Ask children to listen for names of siblings, cousins or friends.
- Talk about interesting or funny things that happened in your class last year.
- Give a tour of the school and grounds. Point out any changes.
- Introduce staff members.
- Set aside a question and answer period. Encourage children to express their concerns. This can be a written activity for older students.
- When time is available, hold individual conferences.

Have all classroom furniture ready for use. Make sure books and other materials are visible.
- Play an appropriate ice-breaking game.
- As soon as possible after children arrive, explain the daily schedule.
- Have at least one homelike spot in the room. You can include a rocking chair, a colorful plant, a goldfish, rug, toy or framed picture.
- Encourage children to help you as much as possible. They can run errands, distribute and gather paper and materials, and prepare supplies.

GENEVIEVE BYLINOWSKI

Desk Name Tags

Colorful desk name tags can be made from multicolored graphlike contact paper. Write each child's name on this lined plastic with a permanent black marker. Cut the tag out, peel and stick. This works better than laminated sentence strips. These tags will brighten students' desks year-round.

KENNETH HELMS

Special Delivery

Make a large blue mailbox, mailman and a large white residential mailbox from construction paper or by coloring plain white paper. Post them on the board. Write each child in your class a personalized letter welcoming him or her to school. Include a good luck penny in each letter. Enclose the letters in envelopes. Write the children's names on the envelopes, and include your name and room number in the upper left corner. You may want to stamp the envelopes with a rubber stamp in the upper right corner for a realistic effect. Attach the envelopes to the board with pins so students can remove and read their letters on the first day of school.

PAULA ANDERSON

Start the School Year Right

All Together Now

Use a large piece of white tagboard (24 by 36 inches) to make a class jigsaw puzzle. Divide the tagboard into sections with a pencil, marking off a section for each student in the class. Outline the sections with a black marking pen and cut the pieces apart. Then, on the first day of school, give each student a puzzle piece on which to draw a picture, symbol, or message that tells something about him- or herself. Have students sign their names at the bottom of their puzzle pieces.

Then have kids put the puzzle together. When the puzzle is complete, mount it on the bulletin board and title it "Getting Together," symbolizing the importance of teamwork and class unity.

GRETA ZELLER-MARTIN

A Fitting Welcome

Use this bulletin board idea to let each child know he or she is an important part of the whole group. First, randomly divide the class into teams of four or five students each. For each team, cut a sheet of tagboard into jigsaw-puzzle pieces and mark each piece with a color dot. Use a different color to identify each group. Write each child's name on a separate puzzle piece, matching group members' names with the different colored dots.

On the first day of school, pass out the puzzle pieces and ask students to draw themselves on their sections. Then, ask kids to meet in their color groups to tape the pieces together. Mount completed puzzles on the board. Extend the activity by asking each child to write a brief autobiography, a list of likes and dislikes, or a statement about hobbies, and post along with the self-portraits.

SUE KREIBICH

Here's Looking At You

Welcome students back to school with this playful photo display. Hang a construction-paper cutout of a detective looking through a magnifying glass and attach a caption saying, "I'm looking for a great class!" Place a list of students' names underneath the magnifying glass. At recess, take photographs of each student in your class and replace the list of names with the photos. Change the caption to read, "I've found a great class!"

KATHY JOHNSON

Classroom Helpers

Here's an organizational bulletin board that allows you to "reach out and touch someone" when you need a little help! Make a giant telephone out of black construction paper. Where the numbers would normally be on a telephone, place a circle cut from construction paper with a child's name on it. Make hands with pointing fingers from yellow construction paper. Write a chore on each hand. Use construction paper for telephone cord and receiver. Write "Dial for Help" on receiver. Move hands each week to point at a different person, making sure each student gets a chore for the week.   PAULA MILLENDER GOINES

WHAT'S FOR LUNCH?

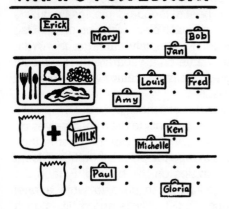

What's For Lunch?

Use a section of your board to take lunch count and attendance in the morning! Have children remove name tags from the top of the board and hang them on one of the three bottom rows, indicating if they are buying lunch, buying milk, or if they packed their lunch. When students are working on their first assignment, simply glance at the board to take attendance and lunch count. Name tags of absentees will remain at the top. Laminate name tags for longer use. Hang tags on cupboard hooks or plastic thumbtacks.

ANGELA N. LOWE

If You're Here, Stick Your Neck Out!

Help children get acquainted and assist roll call. Cut out construction-paper turtle shells and bodies. Make two vertical shell slits. Each student adds name and decoration, and slides the body through the shell. Staple to board. Upon arrival, kids push the tail so the head sticks out. When departing, they do the reverse.   MAUREEN FULLER

In The Spotlight

Leave this bulletin board up until every school star has a chance to take center stage. Staple curtain material to frame the board. During the first week of school, display in the spotlight a picture of yourself and a short paragraph about you. Each week, follow up with a new celeb — a student, secretary, or the principal.

SARA KERR

Cameras As Self-Esteem Tools

Cameras can be important tools for developing self-esteem in the classroom. Any camera will do, and the teacher doesn't have to be a professional photographer.

Take a picture of each child on the first day of school. Mount the pictures on a bulletin board. Group pictures of the children, snapshots of the classroom aides and teacher are included. Keep the display up all year.

Outside the hall or in the classroom, reserve a bulletin board for a brag board. When a child wins an award, writes an outstanding paper, etc., put his or her snapshot on the board.

Put the photos in a scrapbook at the end of the year.

TOBI BANISTER

Birthday Hits

Delight kids with this DJ. Staple a drawn face to the board, add yarn hair. Form a body from discarded clothing. Hang records, and add a list of hits — children's birthdays for the month.

ATLANTA AREA CENTER FOR TEACHERS

Our People

A bulletin board is dedicated to the class all year. Each week is devoted to one person, whose name is printed on a favorite color paper. The person brings in things for the board that describe hobbies, family life, favorite books, foods, pets, sports, awards, etc. On Friday, family and friends of the special person are invited to class. The featured person introduces the guests and explains the board. The first week of school the board features the teacher. School workers and community members can also be featured.

LISA RAE ANDERSON

September

○ All-American Breakfast Month
○ National Cat Health Month
○ National Chicken Month
○ National Courtesy Month

Movable Events

First Monday—Labor Day, to honor all persons who work
Second Sunday—Grandparents Day, to remember these important people
Week after second Sunday—National Hispanic Heritage Week, to recognize and honor those with an Hispanic background
Third Tuesday—UN International Day of Peace, to promote peace among all nations
About September 21—First day of autumn
Fourth Sunday—Good Neighbor Day, to remember next-door friends and neighbors
Fourth Friday—Native American Day, to focus on Native American cultures and traditions
September or October—Rosh Hashanah, Jewish New Year
September or October—Yom Kippur, Jewish Day of Atonement

Red Letter Days

1. The last passenger pigeon died in 1914 at the Cincinnati Zoo. What can you do to help protect endangered species?

2. The U.S. Treasury was founded in 1789. What do you think the colonists used for money before legal currency was established? (They used foreign coins, beaver pelts, grain, nails, and musket balls.)

3. The Treaty of Paris was signed on this day in 1783, marking the end of the Revolutionary War and formally recognizing the United States. Who traveled to France to sign the treaty? (John Adams, Benjamin Franklin, and John Jay)

4. Newspaper Carrier Day. In 1833, Barney Flaherty became the first newsboy in the U.S. He sold *The New York Sun* for a penny. How much does a paper in your community cost today?

5. Be Late for Something Day. But not for school! Maybe for lunch?

6. Jane Addams, who worked for peace, women's rights, and social welfare, was born in 1860. She founded Hull House in Chicago in 1889, one of the first settlement houses in the U.S. What is a settlement house? (A building where programs to help the poor are carried out.)

7. In 1776 a submarine was used for the first time in war. Only one person could fit inside this egg-shaped boat called *The Turtle*. What materials were used to make the sub? How was it operated? (It was made of wood and operated by a hand-cranked propeller.)

8. It's International Literacy Day. To celebrate, read a book. What does literacy mean? (The ability to read and write.)

9. California was the 31st state to join the union in 1850. In what year did your state become a part of the Union? What number was it?

10. Swap Ideas Day. What ideas would you like

to share with the rest of the class? Do you think your ideas are good ones?

11. William Sydney Porter was born in 1862. Using the pen name O. Henry, he wrote many short stories. Most of them had a surprise ending. Read "The Ransom of Red Chief" and enjoy what happened.

12. James Cleveland (Jesse) Owens was born in 1913. One of the most famous athletes in sports history, he won four gold medals in the 1936 Olympics in Berlin, Germany. Read to find out what events he won.

13. Dr. Walter Reed was born in 1851. This physician proved that a mosquito transmitted a deadly disease. What was the disease? (Yellow fever)

14. National Anthem Day. In 1814, Frances Scott Key wrote the words to "The Star Spangled Banner" after watching the British bombardment of Fort McHenry in the Chesapeake Bay. Can you sing it?

15. Agatha Christie, born in 1890, was an author famous for her mysteries. Remember her birthday by borrowing a mystery book from the library.

16. The *Mayflower* departed in 1620 from Plymouth, England with 102 passengers aboard. How do you think people felt about departing for a new world? Would you risk traveling into the unknown for freedom? Why, or why not?

17. Citizenship Day. How does a person not born in the United States become a citizen?

18. The U.S. Air Force became a separate military service in 1947. What are the other U.S. military groups?

19. In 1928, a cartoon starring Mickey Mouse was shown for the first time. Who created this famous film character? (Walt Disney, who also provided Mickey's voice for several years.)

20. Ferdinand Magellan left Spain in 1519 to find a new route to the Spice Islands. One of his ships was the first to circle the globe. Trace its route and find an important strait named for Magellan.

21. Today is World Gratitude Day, planned to unite people in creating a world community. Start a list of what you are grateful for and add one new thing each day for a week.

22. Italo Marchiony applied for a patent for the ice-cream cone in 1903. It was issued on December 15, 1903. What is a patent? (A document granting the exclusive right to produce or sell an invention for a period of time.)

23. In 1846, Neptune was discovered. Where did this planet get its name? Read to find where several other planets got their names. (It is the eighth planet from the sun and is named for Neptune, Roman God of the Sea.)

24. Jim Henson, creator of the Muppets, was born in 1936. What is your favorite Muppet character? Tell why you like it.

25. The Pacific Ocean was first seen by a European in 1513. Vasco Nunez de Balboa saw if from the top of a mountain in what is now Panama. Look up *Balboa* in an encyclopedia and try to find his route to this ocean.

26. Johnny Appleseed was born today in 1774. He received his nickname because he planted apple trees across the midwest. What was his real name? (John Chapman)

27. This is Ancestor Appreciation Day, a day to learn about and appreciate your ancestors. From what country or countries did they come?

28. Confucius' Birthday. Born in China nearly 2,500 years ago, he said, "What you do not wish for yourself, do not do to others." This is his version of the Golden Rule. Why is it called *golden*?

29. Today marks the first public appearance in 1829 of the bobbies of Scotland Yard. In what country is Scotland Yard located? What is it? (It was the first address of the London, England police force and is often used to mean the criminal investigation department of the London police.)

30. Ask a Stupid Question Day. Ask your teacher, librarian, friends, or family a "stupid" question today. You might find that others have the same question and that it isn't so stupid after all.

Apple Madness!

John Chapman, better known as Johnny Appleseed, was born September 26, 1774. He is remembered as a pioneer who planted apple trees all along the American frontier of his time. Join in a September salute to Johnny and apples with these writing ideas!

The Poetry of Apples

Write a haiku about an apple, apple blossoms or apple tree. (Remember that a haiku is a three-line, unrhymed poem with 17 syllables; five syllables in the first line, seven in the second and five in the third.)

Here's an Example:

The ground is covered
With the sweet snow of April
Apple tree blossoms!

Team Time

Apple names include Granny Smith, Winesap, Stayman Winesap, Delicious, Golden Delicious, Cox's Orange Pippin, Rhode Island Greening, Cortland and MacIntosh. Pretend you have just discovered an un-named variety of apple. Work with a partner to name the apple and write a description for it.

National Courtesy Month

Students at Worth Elementary School in Worth, Illinois, start the school year by participating in a special week of courtesy. The guest of honor, Curtis the Courtesy Bee (actually one of the students dressed in full bee regalia), visits each classroom and presents tips on courtesy and good manners. Curtis then politely asks students to write poems and essays, design posters, and prepare skits on what courtesy means to them. The principal also gets in on the act by signing an official Courtesy Week proclamation. Why not proclaim a Courtesy Week in your school?

Dinosaur Manners

Dinosaurs are the craze today, and children love seeing prehistoric creatures in the classroom! Your class will enjoy following in this dinosaur's well-mannered footsteps. Print classroom rules on footprints cut from construction paper. Dinosaur is cut from construction paper and highlighted in black marker. ROSE BORGNA

Courtesy Counts

Emphasize the need to be courteous and kind with a bulletin board display of Elmo the Elephant. Surround Elmo with a peanut holder for each child. Whenever you see a student being especially considerate to another, give the student a paper peanut to put in his or her peanut holder. Once a week, trade paper peanuts for real ones. ELIZABETH STAYE

Labor Day

The first observance of Labor Day—a legal holiday to honor American workers—was organized by Peter J. Maguire, the founder of the United Brotherhood of Carpenters and Joiners, on September 5, 1882, at a parade in New York City. Oregon was the first state to make it a legal holiday in 1887. President Grover Cleveland signed the bill for it in 1894.

Since many schools do not begin until after Labor Day, this holiday is not usually discussed, or even recognized. Many pupils think of it as just one more day of vacation before school starts. Spend a few minutes on the first school day discussing Labor Day's origin, original purpose, when it became a national holiday, and what celebrations were held in your community.

Math Marvels

How can you help students ease back into the school year? Try using their summer experiences as a springboard to mathematics activities.

Construct a class graph of summer activities. First, make a general list of warm-weather activities, such as swimming, horseback riding, camping, family vacations, and so on. Then go around the room and ask each child to share his or her favorite summer activity. List the different categories on the board. As kids reveal what activities they participated in, put a check next to the appropriate categories. Use the graph data to reinforce such concepts as order of numbers, and greater than and less than.

Make a list of the places kids visited during the summer and identify the locations on a map. Have children use a mileage chart, or mileages shown on the map, to determine the distance to each location. Use calculators to determine the total number of miles children traveled during the summer. Round the sum to the nearest hundred miles. Older students can use calculators to compute the average number of miles each class member traveled. Discuss why the average is less than what some children traveled and more than what others traveled.

In pairs or individually, have children make mathematical jigsaw puzzles. First, instruct kids to draw pictures of the most memorable things they did during the summer, then paste their pictures to pieces of poster board. Next, have kids cover their designs with multishaped pattern blocks. How many different shapes can they use to cover the entire area of the picture? Kids then trace around the blocks and cut out the pieces.

HILDE HOWDEN

A Bus Brief

One worry that many youngsters have at the beginning of the year is making sure they get on the right bus. To meet this concern, why not do some role playing?

The children play at riding on the bus and even at accidentally getting on the wrong bus. They then act out problems and solutions, so if the situation really does occur they will better be able to handle it.

One child may ask, "Could I get lost?" Another child may answer with, "Maybe the bus driver could help you find the right bus."

JUNE A. BAILEY

Autumn Begins

Use the change of seasons from summer to autumn as a springboard to a writing activity. Ask kids to imagine what it would be like if the seasons never changed. What would they miss most? And least? If you live in an area where it's always warm, have kids imagine what it would be like if, for instance, there was a sudden snowstorm. Have kids discuss their ideas, then write essays to share with the class.

National Hispanic Heritage Week

National Hispanic Heritage Week is the time we recognize the contributions of Hispanic peoples and cultures from Spain, Portugal and Latin America.

The Bronco Buster Did It

Each of these words came into English from Spanish: bronco, rodeo, sombrero, stampede, lasso, fiesta, pinata, corral, mesa, pinto and patio. Look up the meaning of each word and use the words in a mystery story that takes place at a rodeo.

How Do You Say Yummy in Spanish?

Write a poem praising one of these foods that we've borrowed from Hispanic countries: taco, enchilada, chili, paella, burritos, refried beans, salsa, carne asada or guacamole.

Hispanic Heritage Week

This is a great time to explore the rich history, tradition, and language of Hispanic cultures. Get kids excited about studying Mexico, for example, by having them pretend to be travel agents assigned to promote Mexico. How would they advertise Mexico? What sights and points of interest would they emphasize? Students may wish to design travel brochures, posters, and slogans.

Picture This

Vacations, birthdays, holidays, school memories and the like have all been preserved for years on film. However, it was just about 100 years ago that it first became possible for an ordinary person to take photographs for pleasure. Before this time, cameras were costly and cumbersome, and photography was an expensive and very specialized hobby.

September 4, 1888, marks the day that George Eastman patented his Kodak camera, the forerunner of today's snapshot camera. This camera was preloaded with enough film for 100 exposures and took a round picture 2 1/2 inches in diameter. The camera cost $25 and included a memorandum book for a record of photos taken and a leather carrying case.

Celebrate the anniversary of the snapshot by starting a class photo album. Include class group photos, snapshots of field trips, special class presentations, plays, projects, fairs, and "a day in the life" shots for children working at their desks, playing on the playground, etc.

Name _____

Words, Words, Ole!

Did you know that *banana, macho, patio,* and *stampede* are just a few of many words in the dictionary that are Spanish in origin? See how many more you can find during Hispanic Heritage Week, a time to appreciate the contributions made to the United States by Hispanic-Americans (people whose ancestors came from Spanish-speaking countries). Try these activities, too. They're all about the special flavor that Spanish has added to place names.

Words In Their Place

Take a look at a map of the United States and you'll find many Spanish words. Use this Spanish dictionary to translate the meaning of each city or town. The first one is done for you. (HINT: Sometimes you'll need to change the order of the words.)

1. Rio Grande City (Texas) B i g   R i v e r City
2. Bonita Springs (Florida) __ __ __ __ __ __Ⓞ__Ⓞ Springs
3. Santa Barbara (California) __ __ __ __ __ Barbara
4. Tres Piedras (New Mexico) __ Ⓞ__ __ __ __ __ __ __ __
5. Del Rio (Texas) __ __ __ __ __ __ __ __ __ __ __
6. Buena Vista (New Mexico) __Ⓞ__Ⓞ __ __ __ __ __
7. San Antonio (Texas) __ __Ⓞ__ __ Anthony
8. Pinos Altos (New Mexico) __ __ __ __ __ __ __ __ __ __ __
9. Casa Grande (Arizona) __ __ __ __ __ __ __ __
10. Del Mar (California) __ __ __ __ __ __ __ __Ⓞ

ADD IT UP: Unscramble the circled letters to find the name of the U.S. state that means *full of flowers* in Spanish.

Spanish Dictionary

altos	high	**piedras**	stones
bonita	beautiful	**pinos**	pines
buena	good	**rio**	river
casa	house	**san**	saint (male)
del	of the	**santa**	saint (female)
grande	big	**tres**	three
mar	sea	**vista**	view

Gold Star Idea

★ Choose one of the towns or cities listed above. Look it up on a map. Write directions for driving from where you live to that place.

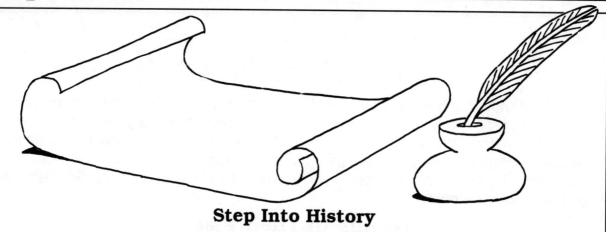

Step Into History

September 17, 1787, is one of the most important dates in American history. On that day, the Constitution of the United States was signed. Write your way into history with these activities.

Extra! Extra!

Imagine you are a newspaper reporter covering the signing of the Constitution. Write a headline and a short news story about the events of September 17, 1787. The story should answer five questions: Who? What? When? Where? Why?

Speak Up

The Constitution did not give blacks or women the right to vote. (Blacks were granted that right in 1870; women in 1920.) Pretend you are a delegate in 1787 and that you believe voting rights should be extended to blacks and women. Write your speech in advance to convince others to agree with your opinion.

Team Time

In a group, discuss what the Preamble, or opening, of the Constitution means. (Look for a copy in an encyclopedia.) Rewrite the Preamble using clear, simple language that young kids can understand.

Room For Improvement

Discuss the nature of political compromise, and raise the subject of the original exclusion of women, blacks, and 18-to-20-year-olds in the voting rights sections of the Constitution. Emphasize the idea that the Constitution is a living document that can be amended and improved. Ask kids to consider this quote by Thomas Jefferson about the Constitution: "I see in this instrument a great deal of good....There are indeed some faults which revolted me a good deal in the first moment: but we must be contented to travel on towards perfection, step by step. We must be contented with the ground this constitution will gain for us, and hope that a favourable moment will come for correcting what is amiss in it."

SHIRLEY GARNER   CHARLOTTE FRANK

Constitution Week

Commemorate the anniversary of the signing of the U.S. Constitution on September 17, 1787, in Philadelphia, Pennsylvania. The Constitution went into effect nine months later, on June 21, 1788, when it was ratified by nine states and replaced the Articles of Confederation.

● Discuss the historical implications surrounding the signing of the U.S. Constitution, then follow up by playing a variation of the game *Jeopardy*—you supply the answers and students must come up with the questions. For example:

● George Washington and James Madison (Which two delegates became U.S. presidents?)

● 39 (How many delegates signed the Constitution?)

● The National Archives Building in Washington, D.C. (Where is the original Constitution kept?)

Our Constitution

● Ask students to research the people who created the Constitution and the Constitutional Convention itself. Read Jean Fritz's *Shh! We're Writing the Constitution* (Putnam, 1987) and check libraries for biographical material about the Constitutional Convention. (Fritz heartily recommends that upper-grade students look at the multi-volume *Dictionary of American Biography.*)

● Ask each child to select a different character and to create a puppet. Together, develop dialogue for a puppet show. Take the puppet show to a hospital, senior citizens' residence, or to another class.

● After studying the Constitution, write your own class constitution, and—muster up your courage—be ready to live by it. To prepare kids to vote on important issues, discuss the purposes of schooling and the tensions between individual rights and the general welfare. Plan to allow for amendments if needed as the year progresses. Together, determine which issues will be decided by class vote and which you alone will decide. What will happen if a child—or you the teacher—violates the constitution? Remember that your goal is to demonstrate the principle of self-government by an informed people.

● Look for local, state, or national issues that your class can form reasonable opinions about. Encourage kids to write letters to newspaper and magazine editors or to government representatives. Take inspiration from Jean Fritz, historian and children's author: "Kids need to really feel like they're participating. It would be great if kids could really do something that would actually change something in America."

● Ask children to imagine that they are the first colonists of a space station. They'll need to create a constitution to help them live together. What do the colonists need to guard against?

What rights do they need to protect? Divide the class into small groups and ask each group to draft a constitution for life at the space station. Together, compare the documents, practice the art of compromise, and vote on a final version.

● If yours is one of the original 13 states, research details of your state's ratification of the Constitution. Who was for it? Who was against? Why? Ask students to create skits about the debates. Then, with kids in costume, videotape the skits. Or students could draw cartoons about the debates. Place the videotape or cartoons in your school library or exchange with another school.

● Invite a newspaper editor to speak about freedom of the press; invite local clergy to speak about freedom of religion; invite a judge, district attorney, or local lawyer to speak about due process. Prepare your speakers by describing your students' ages and comprehension levels.

● Ask bilingual kids—or students learning a foreign language—to make a poster about citizenship or to copy the Bill of Rights in another language. Look for locations to post students' work where residents familiar with the language will see it.

● After reading the first Bill of Rights, invite students to petition your principal or school board. They might ask that a day be designated to honor a certain person or idea, that discretionary school funds be used for a specific purpose, or that a new policy be considered.

● After discussing what it means to be an American citizen, challenge students to prepare a quiz focusing on the basic concepts of citizenship and the Constitution. After making refinements, duplicate it; and ask pupils in other classes to take the quiz. Those who pass it get student-made ribbons reading, "Proud to be a Citizen," or some similar slogan.

SHIRLEY GARNER   CHARLOTTE FRANK

Native American Day

I   stars   go   horse

Celebrate Native American Day with these writing activities.

All About Me

Research the life of a Native American who has made a contribution to history. Pretend you are the person. Write a speech telling about the most important moment in your life. Deliver the speech to the class. (Some possibilities include: Marie Dorion, Pauline Johnson, Chief Joseph, Susette La Flesche, Pocahontas, Sacagawea, Sequoya, Tecumseh and Jim Thorpe.)

A Word from Coyote

Coyote, a character from Native American myths, is clever, proud and able to talk to people and other animals. Write a story about Coyote's adventure at your school.

You may wish to borrow a book from the library about Native American mythology and read about legends from other cultures, such as the Inuit, as well. Compare the legends from the different cultures. Then try writing a legend of your own explaining how the world came to be.

Team Time

Native Americans used pictographs to communicate. For example: I stars go horse. With a friend, create your own pictograph language. Be sure not to let the code fall into anyone else's hands! Send secret messages back and forth.

Teach A Bit Of History Using Totem Poles

Making totem poles in the classroom is a great way to celebrate Native American Day. Try this activity to teach children about the Northwest Coast Indians, who were the original crafters of totem poles.

Totem poles are carved from wood with birds, animals, and fish on them to symbolize an Indian family's characteristics. Some totem poles also have people carved on them. They can be found standing facing the ocean, attached to Indian houses on either side of the doorways, or near burial sites.

Your class can make totem poles using cardboard rolls from paper towels. Ask students to design and cut colorful birds, animals or frightening faces from construction paper. Have the students glue them onto the cardboard rolls vertically.

Extend the activity by using it to develop students' self-esteem. The children can create contemporary symbols for their totem poles which represent a chosen occupation, favorite activity, etc. For example, a swimmer could design a swift shark, a pilot could make an eagle, etc. Display the completed projects around the room and have children try to guess which poles belong to their classmates.

JOAN KAMM   FREYA OTTEM HANSON

Witch Word Scramble

It's a calendar dressed as a word game! Cut out 31 pumpkins. On one side of each pumpkin, print a date and a scrambled word. On the reverse side, print the correct spelling. Each day, a child unscrambles the word and checks the answer.
ATLANTA CENTER FOR TEACHERS

A Walk Through Fall

Bring autumn's colors into your classroom with leaves kids collect during a nature walk. To preserve leaves, wipe them with cooking oil and press between sheets of newspaper. When dry, attach to a construction-paper fall scene.
LAURIE SCHWARTZER

Dye-Dip Leaves

Invite children to create a bulletin board display with leaves they make from paper coffee filters and food coloring. Kids fold filters, then dip edges into different colors of the diluted dye. Press between paper toweling, then cut into leaf shapes and arrange on a door or window.
ANGELA ANDREWS

Fall Reflections

Fold a sheet of paper in half. Paint watercolor trees on the top half, intermittently refolding to create "reflections." Add details to upper trees. Apply a wash to the bottom half, using few strokes to avoid muddying the colors.　SUSAN TINGEY

Fall Bulletin Board

Students help make this fall bulletin board by painting leaves with tempera paints mixed with liquid starch. Dip fabric scraps into the paint and starch mixture. Hang the fabric scraps to dry and stiffen into leaflike shapes. Students also make leaves from colored tissue paper.

Cut a tree trunk from brown butcher paper. Wrinkle and then smooth out to give it a realistic bark look.

Attach the trunk to the board and add the leaves. Place a few leaves near the base. Add a few real leaves to complete the effect.

TAMARA BOWLES

Seasonal house

Decorate a bulletin board with a house that changes with the seasons! Cut a house from a roll of bulletin board paper. Color windows yellow. For Halloween, add a witch, black cats, a jack-o'-lantern on the porch, a ghost, bats, spiders, etc. Change the house's decorations for each holiday.

The house is full of Indians and Pilgrims gathered for a feast in November. In December, real holiday lights decorate the house. A glimpse in the windows reveals children sleeping upstairs, a fire in the fireplace and holiday decorations.

Use your own original ideas to decorate the house throughout the year, changing the decorations to fit a theme each month.

PHYLLIS BOWLING   BETTY TUCKER

Help Is On The Way!

In honor of National Newspaper Week, try this newsworthy bulletin board. First, cover the bulletin board with the help-wanted pages of your local paper. Then create categories of available classroom jobs, such as lunch-count monitor, class messenger, line-up leader, classroom cleanup crew, and so on. After assigning classroom jobs, post students' names under the appropriate categories. Rotate jobs each week.

ATLANTA AREA CENTER FOR TEACHERS

Dear Editor...

Here's the latest scoop—it's National Newspaper Week. Celebrate with this newsworthy writing activity.

People often write letters to the editors of newspapers or magazines to express their opinions on certain subjects. Write your own Letter to the Editor. Let the editor of your school or local newspaper know your opinion on a topic that really matters to you. Remember, your opinion counts!

Fire Prevention Week

To promote fire safety, the National Fire Protection Association offers a comprehensive K-8 Learn Not to Burn curriculum that includes lesson plans, activities, teaching aids, and resources for three levels: Level I—K-2; Level II—grades 3-5; Level III—grades 6-8. To order the Learn Not to Burn curriculum or for more information, contact the National Fire Safety Association, Public Education, One Batterymarch Park, Quincy, MA 02269; (800) 344-3555.

Viking Explorations

While we honor Columbus for his exploration of the New World, historians are sure that the Vikings were the first to sight, land, and create a colony on North America. Ask students to locate, on a world map, Norway, Iceland, Greenland, Newfoundland, and New England to see the relationships among these places. Then have them research the Vikings and their explorations, using the encyclopedia and books from the library.

Questions to Consider

What have archaeologists found in North America to prove the Viking discovery? More than a thousand Viking objects—ranging from iron boat rivets, bronze cloak pins, and a spindle whorl, to three long sod houses at l'Anse aux Meadows on the northern tip of Newfoundland—have convinced scholars. Some researchers believe l'Anse aux Meadows was the site of the Vinland colony.

Could the Spanish have been aware of the ~rse voyages across the North Atlantic? An ~ontroversy persists over whether or not ~us made a secret voyage to Iceland to ~ections across the Atlantic.

~ Norse settlement or settlements ~ fail, when the Vikings were suc~ ~querors and successful colon~ ~ut Europe? European weapon~ ~ the 14th centuries were ~t much ~ose of the Skraelings ~g word ~ and the Indians' boats ~have beer ~ maneuver in inland ~ply lin~ ~ North America and ~re lor ~erous, even during ~s of ~ to 13th centuries. ~de ~ after about 1200, ~ en~ ~ became more pre~ ~d ~ of Columbus's "disc~ ~w ~ Viking colony

in Greenland was abandoned. Norse contact with Native Americans seems to have stopped around the time of the first Spanish colonies in the 16th century.

Activities

Take the class on an imaginary Viking voyage to the New World. Bring in RyKrisp or oatcakes, hard cheese, dried apples, and cranberry juice to help imaginations along.

● Suggest that students pretend they're on a Viking ship. Ask them to keep a journal each day for two weeks, noting the weather and the landscape (or seascape) they see every day, and any interesting events. Challenge the kids to learn some Viking navigation strategies—those that work without the aid of instruments. How can you tell how far north or south you are, how close to the North Pole? First find the North Star. Then determine the height of the North Star above the horizon, measured in terms of a fist held at arm's length. Place one fist above the other. Figure 10 degrees latitude for each fist length needed. Another clue is the length of day in winter.

How can you tell how far you've travelled? The sun comes up earlier or later than expected, but you need accurate clocks to calculate how far you've gone. These were not invented until after the Viking era.

● Vikings were among the greatest shipbuilders of their time. Research the construction of a Viking ship. Why does having a keel matter? What does a rudder do? Make models of clay or Popsicle sticks and sail them to test kids' ideas. Ask students where or when a canoe might be preferable to a Viking ship.

● Archaeologists found a medieval Norwegian coin in Maine. Can children suggest what might be learned from this coin? Ask them to study a U.S. penny. What does it tell about U.S. technology, society, religion, and history?

● Ask your librarian for help in finding photos of Viking art to share with kids. Some of the best known art works were animal ornaments— horse, dog, wolf, lion, or bear stretched and twisted into a fantasy shape filling all the space of a surface. Suggest that the kids explore the style themselves on paper cut in rectangles, squares, circles, ovals, and triangles.

ALISON BROOKS   RUTH SELIG

On Your Mark, Get Set—Discover

Everybody knows who sailed the ocean blue in fourteen hundred and ninety-two—Christopher Columbus! And on October 12, we celebrate his important role in the discovery of North and South America. Tap your own spirit of discovery with these writing adventures.

I Was There

Pretend you are a sailor on the Nina, the Pinta, or the Santa Maria during Columbus' first voyage. Write three entries in a journal: one about the day you set sail from Spain, one about a day in the middle of the trip when you think the ships should turn back, and one about the day a shipmate sights land.

Lights, Camera, History!

Imagine you are a movie director and want to make a movie about a famous explorer. Choose the explorer and learn all you can about his or her life. Then choose the movie star you want to play the part. Write a letter persuading the star to play the role.

Team Time

Work in a group to write and perform this skit. Pretend an explorer from the past arrives in the present and applies to NASA for a job as an astronaut. Think about what the NASA interviewer might ask the explorer and what the explorer might say about his or her qualifications.

Smooth Sailing

Commemorate Christopher Columbus's discovery of the New World with the following activity.

On August 3, 1492, Christopher Columbus and his crew set out from Palos, Spain, to find a short sea route to the Indies. Three vessels, the Niña, the Pinta, and the Santa Maria, were prepared for the voyage. After three long weeks at sea, the sailors were weary and wanted to turn back. Fortunately, Columbus persuaded his crew to carry on. So, if you were Columbus, how would you have convinced your crew to continue the journey?

All About Names

We celebrate Columbus Day to commemorate his landing in the New World. At one time, some people wanted to honor Columbus for his discovery by calling our country Columbia. That didn't happen. But Columbus and Columbia are the names of many places around the United States. Think about place names and the people behind them with these writing activities.

What's in a Name?

Make a list of places in your state that are named after people. Research one. Write a paragraph telling about the place you chose and who it is named for.

After You

Imagine that you could build a city named after you! You might call it Amy Falls, Jason City or Loriville. Draw a map of the town and write a paragraph telling what is special about it.

Team Time

Work as a team to create a then-and-now mural. Show what the land on which your town in built might have looked like when Columbus discovered America in 1492. Then show what it looks like today. Write a paragraph to describe each part of the mural.

How Time Flies

On the last Sunday in October, we go back to standard time. How? We turn our clocks back an hour. That means it gets darker earlier in the evening. Take a minute to think about minutes with these writing ideas.

Timely Words

The phrase *in the nick of time* means barely enough. The phrase *a split second* means a very short time. Make a list of other everyday phrases that have to do with time. Next to each phrase, write the definition.

Clock Talk

Imagine that you are a clock or some other modern timepiece. You could be a cuckoo clock, a digital clock, etc. Write a rhymed or unrhymed poem about your life. Tell what you like or don't like about your job. Describe what it's like to be watched by people all day long. Share your personal feelings about what it means to make the most of time.

Team Time

Work in a group to create a time line showing the devices people have used to tell time over the centuries. Write a sentence or two about each device.

Dictionary Delights

Noah Webster was born on October 16, 1758. He compiled the first American dictionary, published in 1828. Celebrate his feat with these writing ideas.

Dictionary Doodle

Look at these dictionary doodles:

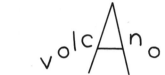 

Note how the shapes and order of the letters signal the meanings of the words. Thumb through a dictionary and look for a word to make into a doodle.

Put Yourself on the Page

Some words come from the names of people. The word *sandwich* is named for the English Earl of Sandwich, who is said to have suggested putting a piece of meat between two slices of bread. Imagine you have invented something. Name it after yourself, and write a definition of it.

Team Time

Do kids you know use special words with each other—like *grody, boss,* and *fresh*? With some friends, write a short dictionary of words that are popular at your school. Include pronunciations and sample sentences.

Get Inventive!

What do the electric light, coast-to-coast telegraph messages and ball-point pens have in common? They're all parts of October history. Find out more in these inventive writing ideas.

Bright Idea

Thomas Edison invented the electric light on October 21, 1879, and people called him a genius. Edison himself defined genius as "one percent inspiration and 99 percent perspiration." What do these words tell us about Edison's belief about hard work? Share your beliefs by writing your own definition of genius, success, failure and inspiration. Use a dictionary to get started.

Send a Message!

On October 24, 1861, a telegraph line from the East to the West coast was completed. Write a special message you would like to send in a telegram to a friend, relative or the president.

Team Time

Imagine that a pencil, a ball-point pen (patented on October 30, 1888) and a computer could talk. Write a skit using the writing tools as characters. Have each character explain how it changed the world. Invent a future writing tool. Have the new invention tell what it can do and how it will change the world in the skit. Perform the skit for your class.

Parts Of Speech Spider

Kids will have lots of creepy fun with this parts-of-speech bulletin board. First, make an eight-legged spider cutout, complete with eyes and feet. Label each foot with a different part of speech: noun, pronoun, verb, adverb, adjective, preposition, conjunction, and interjection. Then print the classifications for each part of speech on brightly-colored construction-paper shoes. When studying pronouns, for example, make shoes for subjective, possessive, and objective; a unit on nouns would include singular, plural, common, proper, subject and direct object. Attach the shoes to the backs of the respective feet. When discussing a part of speech bring the shoes to the front.

GERALDINE M. ANDERS

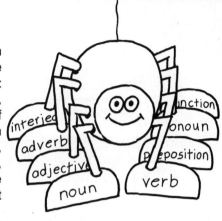

Halloween Read-Along

Keep everyone in your reading group following along with Halloween fingertips. During October, each child wears a Halloween fingertip, or "pointer," on the index finger while reading. "Dracula nails" or long, red fingernails are inexpensive and readily available at this time of the year. Children love using them, and the teacher can tell at a glance if they are following.

ELLEN GARB

Halloween Nouns

One trick to expanding kids' vocabulary is to treat them to this Halloween bulletin board. Ask students to think of holiday-related nouns and to print them on individual slips of paper. Kids attach words to the haunted-house background, then use them in original Halloween stories.　　　JANET LEWIS

Create-A-Witch

Here's a writing activity to capture the Halloween spirit. First, have kids write paragraphs that describe witches. Collect the paragraphs and ask children to share them with the class. Because it's likely that many kids will describe witches as wicked, wizened characters who wear black hats and ride brooms, you might suggest to the class that perhaps there are other ways to describe witches. How about a witch in a jogging suit? A witch with red hair wearing a polka-dot dress? A male witch (warlock) in a tuxedo and cowboy hat? Ask kids for other wacky suggestions and list them on the board. Armed with lots of way-out ideas, have kids describe witches again—this time from a new, more creative perspective.　　　KAREN HIMMEL

4 November

○ Aviation History Month
○ Child Safety and Protection Month

Movable Events

First Tuesday after first Monday—General Election Day

Second full week—Children's Book Week, to focus on new books for children

Second full week—National Geography Awareness Week

Week preceding Thanksgiving—American Education Week

Thursday before Thanksgiving—Great American Smoke Out, to promote nonsmoking

Fourth Tuesday—Thanksgiving

Week ending with Thanksgiving Day—National Farm-City Week, to cement relations between city and country

Week including Thanksgiving—National Family Week, to promote family ties

Last full week—Latin American Week, to promote relations with Latin American countries

---

Red Letter Days

1. National Authors Day. Who is your favorite author?

2. Spruce Goose Flight. This huge airplane, made of plywood, was the world's largest plane in 1947 when it made its first and only flight—about one mile and at an altitude of 70 feet. Read to find out about this plane.

3. It's Sandwich Day, in honor of the inventor the Fourth Earl of Sandwich, born in England in 1718. Invent a sandwich and name it after yourself.

4. King Tut's tomb was discovered in 1922. What did its contents tell us about life in Ancient Egypt?

5. Guy Fawkes Day—a day of festivities and bonfires in England, to celebrate the arrest of the conspirators who planned to blow up the Houses of Parliament and King James I in 1605. Read to find out who these people were.

6. Adolphe Sax (1814) and John Philip Sousa (1854) were born on this day. Both invented musical instruments that were named after them. What were they? Describe them.

7. Marie Curie was born in 1867. Read to find out why everyone should be thankful for her work and discoveries.

8. Merchant Sailing Ship Preservation Day. In 1941, the whaling ship *Charles W. Morgan,* arrived in Mystic, Connecticut. This was the first of many old commercial ships that have been saved and restored so that today we can see how these ships looked and were used. Is there a restored ship near you? Have you visited it?

9. On this day in 1965, a massive power failure cut the electric power in much of northeastern United States and Ontario and Quebec in Canada. More than 30 million persons were affected. Talk to an older person who remembers this blackout.

10. The U.S. Marine Corps was founded in 1775. Do you know why? Read to find out.

11. Today is Veterans Day, honoring the men

and women who fought in wars for our country. Pay tribute to these brave people by writing a special poem, visiting a veterans' hospital, or sending a letter to a person in the service.

12. Elizabeth Cady Stanton, born in 1815, worked hard for women's suffrage. Which amendment to the Constitution guarantees women the right to vote?

13. The author Robert Louis Stevenson was born in 1850. Find a copy of his book *A Child's Garden of Verses.* Select a poem you like, and learn a few lines of it.

14. Claude Monet, a French painter, was born in 1840. He is famous for painting the same scene at different times of the day or year. Do a sketch of an outdoor scene in the morning and again in the afternoon. How are they different?

15. Shichi-Go-San. This Japanese children's festival is one of the most picturesque events of autumn. Parents thank the guardian spirits for the healthy growth of their children and prayers are offered for their further development. List some of the things you are thankful for and some things you hope for in the future.

16. W. C. Handy was born in 1873. This American composer and bandleader was called "the Father of the Blues." Ask your music teacher to play some blues music for you.

17. Homemade Bread Day. Ask your mom or dad if you can make some bread this weekend.

18. In 1928 Mickey Mouse, his squeaky voice, and animated actions first appeared in *Steamboat Willie,* shown at the Colony Theater in New York City. It was the first animated talking picture. Find out how an animated cartoon is made.

19. On this day in 1863, there were two speeches made at the dedication of a Civil War cemetery in Gettysburg, Pennsylvania. One speech was two hours long, the other two minutes. Yet it is the two-minute one we remember. Who made the shorter speech?

20. Chester Gould was born in 1900. This popular cartoon artist created the *Dick Tracy* comic strip and drew and wrote it from its first appearance in 1931 until 1977. Have you ever created a comic strip? Try it.

21. World Hello Day. To be an active participant in this day, you must say hello to at least 10 people.

22. In 1935 a "flying boat" called the *China Clipper* left San Francisco to begin regular airmail service across the Pacific. Nearly 60 hours later the big ship landed at Manila in the Philippines. By the next October the plane was carrying passengers as well as mail. Why was it called a "flying boat?" Look up the topic *aviation* in an encyclopedia to find out.

23. The Female Medical Educational Society of Boston, Massachusetts was founded in 1848 "to provide and promote the education of midwives, nurses, and female physicians...." But here's the surprise—its officers were all men. Why would it have been necessary to have such a society?

24. What simple invention did Joseph F. Glidden receive a patent for in 1874. (Barbed wire) How did this invention make possible the settlement of the frontier by small farmers and help to bring about the end of the open range method of cattle grazing?

25. Joe DiMaggio, born in 1914, was one of the greatest outfielders in baseball history. List some of your favorite baseball players. What positions do they play?

26. The first black person to speak out against slavery was a woman who took the name Sojourner Truth. No one knows her birthday so we remember her on the anniversary of her death in 1883. She was called an abolitionist because of her views. What is an abolitionist?

27. There was great excitement in Stratford-on-Avon, England in 1759. A church vicar and his wife had been living in Shakespeare's home, where there was a tree planted by Shakespeare himself. So many people came to see the tree that the annoyed couple cut it down. On this day the town corporation immediately ejected the couple from Stratford for one of "the meanest petty infamies in our annals." Why, do you think, the town was so upset?

28. William Blake, the English poet, was born in 1757. You will like to read *The Tiger,* a handsome book of one of his poems.

30. Samuel Clemens was born in 1835. We know this American writer by his more familiar pen name, Mark Twain. Research where he got his pen name, how he felt about Halley's Comet, and find the name of one of his books.

November

Aviation History Month

Encourage students to let their imaginations soar with this high-flying creative writing exercise. Have kids select famous people from aviation history who they'd most like to have flown with, such as the Wright brothers, or Charles Lindbergh, then write essays telling why. Have students share their essays with the class.

Shichi-Go-San

If you were in Japan on November 15, you might see people celebrating Shichi-Go-San, a holiday that honors 3-, 5-, and 7-year old children. Three-year-olds are honored because they are no longer considered babies, 5-year-olds because they are no longer toddlers, and 7-year-olds because they are on their way to being grown up.

Challenge your class to fashion a similar holiday that Americans might celebrate. What ages and stages would kids single out as milestones in the process of growing up? As they plan, children might want to research how Shichi-Go-San is celebrated.　AMANDA RAE

Great American Smokeout

Help kids encourage their loved ones to kick the habit with the following activities.
● Make "You Can Do It!" cards encouraging smokers to quit.
● List reasons why people should stop smoking; give copies of the list to smokers you know.
● Create an anti-smoking poster and a slogan to go with it.
● Contact your local affiliate of the American Cancer Society for more information.

Where There's Smoke...

The Great American Smokeout is sponsored by the American Cancer Society to encourage smokers to quit this unhealthy habit. Observe the event with these "kick-the-habit" writing ideas.

Make a Switch

Find a cigarette advertisement in a magazine. Write down all the words or phrases in the ad that make smoking seem appealing. Below each, write what you know about what really happens when someone smokes. For example: *"Cigarettes are cool and refreshing!" "Cigarettes give you bad breath!"*

Ask a Smoker

Take a poll of adult smokers you know. Ask questions like: *When and why did you begin smoking? What advice would you give to a young person who is thinking about smoking? Will you join the Great American Smokeout this year?* Write up your findings for the class.

Team Time

Work with a friend to create an anti-smoking poster. Think of a slogan, like "To smoke is no joke!" Then decide on how to illustrate the slogan. Ask your teacher if you may display your poster in a hallway or in the cafeteria.

To Smoke is NO joke!

Flag Focus

Because many schools are closed by Flag Day in June, the American flag is often ignored as a learning tool. Yet this symbol of our country is important to learn about. Use Veteran's Day to try some of these activities for a flag unit.

1. Discuss and practice proper flag etiquette. List and post several pertinent rules for students to review.

2. Discuss the origin of the flag and its symbolism. Read the following explanation of the flag's design by George Washington: "We take the stars and blue union from heaven, the red from our mother country, separating it by white stripes, thus showing we have separated from her, and the white stripes shall go down to posterity representing liberty." Ask students to design a flag for the class or your school, keeping in mind the importance of symbolism.

3. Have students make replicas of several early American flags. Display them on a wall and discuss how they depict the westward growth of the nation.

4. Print story problems on construction paper stars using statistics (dates, number of stars, number of stripes, etc.) pertinent to American flags both past and present. The stars can be displayed on a bulletin board for students to read and solve throughout the day.

5. Surround the flag with adjectives students suggest to describe it, including majestic, glorious, fluttering, etc.

6. Research flags from other countries. Invite guests from other countries to discuss the customs, origins, history and holidays connected with their flags.

7. Play "Flag Trivia." Each day of the school week, present students with trivia questions pertaining to the flag. Students locating the correct information earn star stickers.

8. Divide the class into teams to look up difficult words used in the Pledge of Allegiance, such as allegiance, republic, indivisible, etc. The class can also look up words from the "Star Spangled Banner."

9. Have students write their congressperson requesting free pamphlets or information available about the flag.

KONNIE MEYER

Let's Remember

November 11 is Veterans Day, honoring men and women of the armed forces who have fought for our country. Salute our veterans with these writing activities.

In Memory of

Design a monument to honor our veterans. Then write a paragraph telling why you believe the monument is a good tribute to them. Describe the materials you would use to make the monument and where you would locate it.

What Makes a Good Citizen?

Veterans are loyal citizens who have risked, and often lost, their lives for their country. Write a paragraph explaining good citizenship. Write about the rights and responsibilities of a loyal citizen.

Team Time

Work with a partner to create a card to send to your local veteran's hospital or organization. In your message, thank the veterans for all they've done.

November

Open House Blues

Whenever groups of parents come to your school, you're bound to hear the same questions over and over. At your next open house try placing informational signs, which can be decorated by the students, on the walls. These signs can answer frequent questions such as, "How much is milk?" "Where is the office?" and "Where is the bathroom?"
SUE WEBER

I made something for you to see. Will you make something for me?

It is fun at our house!
Good job Sheryl
Love, Mom and Dad

A Secret Message

Here's an open house idea that involves sharing between parents and children. First, attach butcher paper along one wall of your classroom. On the top write the following poem: *I made some things for you to see. Will you make something special for me?*

Ask children to draw pictures and write brief messages below the poem, then sign their names. When parents and guests come to open house later that day, they'll be pleasantly surprised to see messages left for them. In return, ask guests to leave messages for the children, such as "We're so proud of you, Joey! We loved your cat picture. Keep up the good work! Love, Mom and Dad."
LINDA MARTIN MERCER

School Is Cool!

American Education Week is a time people have set aside to salute our nation's schools and their important place in our society. Where would you be without school? Think about it with these writing ideas.

Fast Forward
You know all about what school is like right now, but what will school be like in the year 2000? Will kids stay home and work at computers? Will children in space-shuttle schools circle the planet while playing on gravity-free playgrounds? Push the fast-forward button in your brain and write a paragraph describing a school of the future.

Take a Break
Wouldn't someone you know like to take a break from homework? Imagine a homework machine, then write an advertisement to convince kids to buy one. Include a drawing of your invention and a description of how it works.

Team Time
What are you proud of about your school? Do you have a great band? Are your teachers the best? Let your neighborhood know all the good things going on in your school. Work with some buddies to make a poster, write a letter to a local newspaper, or send an announcement to a local radio station.

Getting To Know Us

Here's a get-acquainted activity to welcome guests to your classroom during open house. First, divide the bulletin board into sections and give each student a section. Ask kids to write paragraphs about themselves and their families, including information on hobbies, favorite foods, pets, and so on, then post the paragraphs on the board. Children can further personalize their sections by including photos of their pets, homes, families, even themselves as babies. Parents and guests will enjoy meeting their children's classmates through words and pictures.
HELEN SCHMIDT

November

Making Headlines

Nellie Bly was a famous American newspaper reporter who got a great idea after reading the book *Around the World in 80 Days*. On Nov. 14, 1889, she set out from New York to prove she could travel around the world in less than 80 days! She did it—in 72 days, 6 hours and 11 minutes! Make your own headlines with these writing activities.

"Tell Me, Miss Bly..."
Write an interview with Nellie. First, think of five questions. Then write the answers you think Nellie might have given. Why do you think she would have answered the way you predicted?

I Did it!
What is your greatest accomplishment? What would you like to be known for? Write a newspaper story telling about one of your real or imaginary achievements. Make sure your story has a headline and tells who, what, when, where, and why.

Team Time
Work in groups to find out what was in the news in the year you were born. Look for the information in almanacs and ask the librarian for help. Create a newspaper "front page," summarizing what you discover.

Talk About The Weather

In the past 100 years, weather forecasting has become a more exact science. In the United States, the first national forecasting agency was organized in 1870. The first observations were made on November 1. Write up a storm with these activities.

Weather Symbols
You've probably seen these familiar weather symbols on the news:

rain

high pressure

clear skies

partly cloudy

Create some weather symbols of your own for these conditions: hurricane, dust storm, frost, lightning and fog.

Eye on the Sky
Keep a science log for a week. Record what the sky looks like each evening and what the weather is like the following morning. Based on your findings, can you make predictions about weather by looking at the evening sky? Write your conclusions for the class. Sailors and farmers relied heavily on weather conditions and have many sayings about how to predict the weather. See how many of these sayings you can uncover. Then write modern versions of them.

Team Time
Work as a group to write and illustrate a story about someone who faces a problem because of a weather condition. (Remember Dorothy and Toto's tornado.) Share your story. Try acting out the story as a skit. What kind of sound effects can you use to depict the weather condition in the story?

November

Trotting The Globe

It's Geography Awareness Week. Take a look at the world around you, starting with the following activity.

You are a foreign news correspondent and you've just been asked to research—and visit—a country of your choice. Pick a location on the world map, then write about a well-known historical site, tradition, or special event in that country. Where will you go when you get there? What will you write about?

Celebrating Geography Week

Celebrate Geography Awareness Week with these activity ideas.

● Place a large world map on a bulletin board surrounded by note cards with names of countries written on them. Caption the board, "Where in the world?" Staple yarn to each picture, with the other end of the yarn tied in a loop. Supply large-headed straight pins for children to pin the loop to the spot on the map where they think the country is located. Disassemble daily so all students can have a turn.

● Play the world or state geography game. Use a wall-size map. Divide the class into two teams. A player from each team goes to the map. You give the name of a city, state, country, river, etc. The first person to find it earns a point for his or her team.

● Ask someone to bring in his or her stamp collection. Ask students to find the stamps' countries on the globe.

● Ask community people who have visited or lived in other parts of the world to speak to your class.

● Take the class for a walk around the school grounds or community. Divide students into small groups and have them draw poster-sized maps of what they saw. Compare the finished products and discuss similarities and discrepancies.

● Help students learn the difference between a state, country, continent, etc., by making a bulletin board with the extended address of the school. Title it "We go to school at...Street — City — State — Country — Continent — Hemisphere — Planet." Then, under each caption, give the exact school address.
RENATE WEHTJE

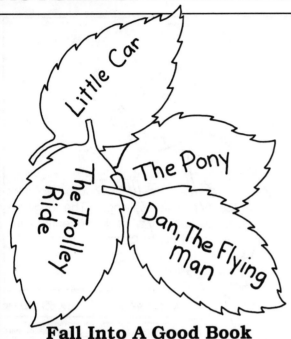

Fall Into A Good Book

Here's a bulletin-board idea to highlight Children's Book Week. Cover the board with yellow butcher paper and trim with a harvest-time border. Attach a cutout tree with construction-paper leaves, then print titles of students' favorite books on the leaves. Next to the tree, attach a reading progress chart on which kids are to note the number of books they've read throughout the year. Title the board "Fall into a Good Book."

MARY WILLIAMS

Book Of The Year

Generate some excitement during Children's Book Week with your own awards presentation. Ask kids to create a name for your book awards, then decide on categories, such as Best Book, Best Male Character, Best Female Character, Best Hero, Best Villain, and Best Author. Each student then chooses one book to read and review. He or she creates a poster listing nominations for up to three awards from the chosen book.

Ask the class to read each poster, then vote by secret ballot on each award. Plan an awards ceremony, complete with presenters who read nominations for a category, then pull the winner's name from an envelope. The child who nominated the winner can make the acceptance speech.

GENE MENICUCA

Children's Book Week

Encourage star storytellers to sparkle by forming a storytelling club in your school. Not only will children develop oral communication skills, they'll also learn to appreciate and enjoy folktales, fairy tales, fables, myths, and legends in a comfortable, nonthreatening environment. Advertise the club in the school newspaper or on a prominent bulletin board. Then have fun telling tall tales!

Reading Comes Alive!

To highlight Children's Book Week, try this bulletin board that combines language arts and crafts. Have students design dust jackets for books they've recently read and have written reports on. Next, have kids make dolls from construction paper and material scraps depicting favorite characters from their books. Post the reports, book jackets, and dolls on the board and title it "Help These Characters Come Alive— Read!"

KATHLEEN KAY

Boundless Books

Once upon a time there was a colorful book diorama...For each one you'll need a cigar box, a 9-by-12-inch sheet of white paper, construction paper, felt-tip markers, fabric scraps, and yarn. To transform the box into a book, cover the top, sides, and bottom with white paper. Draw horizontal lines along the edges to resemble a book's pages. Decorate the outside of the box with markers and construction paper; inside, attach cutout characters. Adorn the characters with fabric scraps, yarn and buttons. Print a familiar quote from the book on the inside cover. Group the dioramas together and proudly display them in your classroom.

CONNIE GATLEY

November

Thanksgiving Day

Observed as an annual United States holiday, the fourth Thursday in November is set aside to recall the three-day celebration feast that took place in Plymouth, Massachusetts, in 1621, now known as Thanksgiving.

To share the Thanksgiving spirit, go around the room and ask kids to describe some of their family Thanksgiving Day traditions. Follow up the discussion with a journal-writing period in which students write about one particularly memorable Thanksgiving Day in their lives.

The Mayflower Compact

On November 21, 1620, the Pilgrims anchored off the coast of Massachusetts. But before they got off the boat, they signed the *Mayflower Compact,* America's first charter for self-government.

Ask kids to imagine themselves as pilgrims who had just reached an unknown shore. What would their concerns be? Remind kids that the *Mayflower Compact* was drawn up a full year before the first Thanksgiving. The original document was lost, but what do students think might have been included in the agreement? Ask them to write their own charter—as Pilgrims long ago or as modern-day pilgrims about to settle a New World. FLORENCE ZIMMERMAN

Turkey Placecards

Your class can make colorful Thanksgiving placecards with handprint turkeys on both sides of folded pieces of construction paper. Have children paint their palms brown, thumbs red, and fingers (feathers) different colors. Then have them make prints next to their names on the cards. Older children can add felt pen details after paint dries.

Our Thanksgiving Tree

At the beginning of November, my students create an ongoing hallway display to share with the entire school community. They write paragraphs describing the things they're particularly thankful for on construction-paper leaves, then attach the leaves to the tree. Afterwards, children draft an open letter to their schoolmates, requesting contributions of thankful thoughts for the hallway tree. By the time Thanksgiving Day arrives, the tree is overflowing with thoughts of thanks. What a nice holiday tradition. LYNNE KENNEDY JOHNSTON

Letters Back Home

Here's a Thanksgiving Day writing activity that integrates language arts and social studies.

Have children pretend they are Pilgrims on the *Mayflower* who are just arriving in America. Their grandparents in England are awaiting letters about the trip. Have kids write letters, choosing one aspect of the long voyage to illustrate. Compile the letters in a class book called *Letters to Our Grandparents from Room _____'s Pilgrims.*

As a follow-up, repeat the activity using information about the Pilgrims' first year in the New World. Include the first Thanksgiving, hardships during the winter, and other relevant, historic details.

KIMBERLY SPRING   SHIRLEY BAIRD

November

Thank You, Mr. Lincoln

Gobble, gobble—it's Thanksgiving. Here's a writing activity to be thankful for. In 1863, after nearly 40 years of hard work, a woman named Sarah Josepha Hale persuaded President Abraham Lincoln to make Thanksgiving Day a national holiday. If you were Hale, what would you have said to persuade Lincoln to make Thanksgiving a national day of thanks?

Giving Thanks

It's Thanksgiving, time to give thanks for our blessings. Count your blessings with these writing activities.

T is For...

Write the letters in the word "Thanksgiving" vertically on a piece of paper, one letter to a line. Then write the names of things you are thankful for that begin with that letter. The first line might say "television, turkey or toys."

You are Cordially Invited

If you could invite someone to share Thanksgiving dinner, who would it be? Write an invitation to the person. Explain why you are inviting him or her.

Team Time

What does Thanksgiving look, sound, smell, and feel like? Work with a partner to create a Thanksgiving picture and word collage. Cut out pictures of food, people and nature from old magazines that remind you of Thanksgiving. Glue the pictures on a sheet of paper. Write description words like spicy, sizzling, etc. near the appropriate pictures. Or, cut words from a magazine and glue them next to the picture.

Name

Pilgrim's Progress

It is September 9, 1620. You are a Pilgrim planning a journey from England to America on the *Mayflower.* The voyage will take about seven to eight weeks, and you can only take a limited number of provisions with you. Your task is to look through the following list of items and rank them in order of importance to survival, both on the voyage to America and during the long months ahead. Decide which items are most important and number them from 1 to 10. Then decide which items are least important and cross them off your list. KATHY FAGGELLA

_____ a suit of armor
_____ a hunting/guard dog
_____ a musket (gun)
_____ 10 lbs. of musket powder
_____ 40 lbs. of lead musket balls
_____ a sword
_____ an axe
_____ a hoe
_____ a hammer
_____ a shovel
_____ an iron cooking pot
_____ 2 bushels of oatmeal
_____ a bushel of sugar and spices
_____ a bushel of salt
_____ a cask of fresh water
_____ an extra set of clothes (shirt, skirt/pants, shoes, coat, stockings)
_____ a set of bedding (canvas sheets and wool blanket)
_____ 8 bushels of wheat flour
_____ a gallon of cooking oil
_____ a set of wooden plates, dishes, and spoons
_____ packets of seeds for gardening
_____ money
_____ a small amount of food packed in a box (cheese, bacon, beef preserved in vinegar, dried fruits)
_____ 4 live chickens (3 hens and a rooster)
_____ a package of herbs used as medicines

5 December

○ Bingo's Birthday Month (the game was invented in 1929)
○ Universal Human Rights Month

Movable Events

November or December—Hanukkah, eight-day Jewish festival of lights
Third Friday—Underdog Day, to salute those number-two people who contribute so much to the number-one people we hear about, such as Robinson Crusoe's Friday or the Lone Ranger's Tonto
About December 21—winter begins
The seven days before to the seven days after the winter solstice—Calcyon days, named after a fabled bird who was thought to calm the wind and waves—a time of peace and tranquility

---

Red Letter Days

1. Rosa Parks Day. In 1955, a tired black woman named Rosa Parks refused to give up her bus seat to a white man in Montgomery, Alabama. Discuss what happened.

2. The first reindeer to be purchased from Russia arrived in Alaska in 1892. Look up this amazing animal and find out why the U.S. purchased these animals.

3. In 1967, the first successful heart transplant operation was performed. Who performed the surgery? Where was it done?

4. The first agricultural society of importance to this country was founded in 1867. Called *the Grange,* its original purpose was to inform farmers of new farming methods. Look up the history of this important organization and read what it accomplished.

5. Happy Birthday, Jim Plunkett. This excellent football player was born in 1947. Ask your librarian for a biography of a favorite sports figure.

6. It's St. Nicholas Day, honoring a fourth-century bishop from Partara, Turkey. What Christmas custom dates back to St. Nicholas?

7. Pearl Harbor Day. In 1941, the Japanese bombed Pearl Harbor in Hawaii, causing great damage and killing many people. What did Congress vote to do the next day?

8. The first greeting card, designed by John Calcott Horsley, was printed in 1843. Start today to make some holiday cards to send or give to friends.

9. In 1886, Clarence Birdseye was born. On a trip to Labrador, he noticed that quickly frozen fish were fresh and flavorful when they thawed out. This gave him an idea. What food process do you think he started? Read to see if your guess was right.

10. A Swedish chemist who invented dynamite is best known for the prizes given each year in his name. Money from his estate is given to the persons who are judged to have made the most valuable contributions to the good of humanity. Prizes are awarded on the anniversary of his death in 1896. Who is this person? What are the prizes given? (Alfred Nobel; peace, literature, chemistry, physics, medicine)

11. In 1901, Guglielmo Marconi sent a morse code

radio signal across the Atlantic for the very first time. Send a secret message to a friend.

12. Poinsettia Day observes the death, in 1851, of Dr. Joel Roberts Poinsett. This American diplomat introduced the plant named for him into the U.S. What is this plant?

13. Today is St. Lucia Day, a Swedish celebration in which the oldest girls rise very early, put on long, white dresses, and serve coffee and buns to their families, before the others are out of bed. Perhaps your family would like to celebrate St. Lucia Day.

14. In 1911, Roald Amundsen and four companions located and visited the South Pole, the first people to do so. What problems must they have had in finding and reaching this spot?

15. Every year since 1900, a census of winter bird life has begun on this day. Count the birds you see on your way home from school today.

16. On this day in 1773, The Boston Tea Party was held. Research this important event.

17. Aviation Day. Take this opportunity to learn about airplanes.

18. Born in 1778, Joseph Grimaldi has been called the greatest clown in history. Celebrate by making someone laugh today.

19. The anthropologist Richard Leakey was born in 1944. What is an anthropologist?

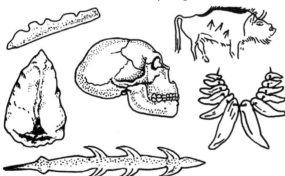

20. In 1803, the U.S. purchased the Louisiana territory from France. More than one million square miles were obtained for about $20.00 per square mile. With 640 acres to a square mile, how much did the U.S. pay per acre?

21. In 1620, the Pilgrims reached Plymouth and stepped foot on land. About how many weeks had they been traveling?

22. "Colo," weighing 3 1/4 pounds, was born at the Columbus, Ohio Zoo in 1956. This was the first gorilla born in captivity. Read to find out about gorillas. Is there one at a zoo near you?

23. In 1987 a plane landed in California after a journey of 24,986 miles. The *Voyager* had taken off on December 14 and returned on this day after making a non-stop flight around the world without refueling. Their flight lasted 216 hours. How many miles per hour was that?

24. Kit Carson, born in 1809, was a famous American hunter, guide, and soldier. He led many exploring parties through the West to the Pacific Coast. Why would people have needed guides in those days?

25. Christmas! Have a happy one!

25. Clara Barton, born in 1821, is best remembered as the founder of the American Red Cross. What does the Red Cross do?

26. The first day of Kwanzaa. This American black family observance has been held since 1966, in recognition of African harvest festivals. Kwanzaa means "first fruit." Read to find out more about this holiday.

27. What do pasteurization, vaccination, and rabies vaccine have in common? All were invented or developed by Louis Pasteur, born in 1822. Select one of these topics and find out why it is important for good health.

28. "A penny saved is a penny earned." Who said that? Benjamin Franklin, who began to publish his *Poor Richard's Almanack* in 1732. Many sayings from the almanack are still remembered today. Make a list of some of them.

29. An accident by Charles Goodyear, born this day in 1800, resulted in an important discovery for the rubber industry. Look up *rubber* in an encyclopedia and read about vulcanization.

30. Rudyard Kipling, born in 1865, wrote many short stories and novels for adults, but his most popular ones were for children. Get a copy of his *Just So Stories* and read his idea of how a leopard got its spots or how the elephant got its trunk.

31. New Year's Eve. In some parts of Ecuador, each family member gives an item of clothing to make a straw man that represents the Old Year. Does your family have a New Year's Eve tradition? Describe it.

December

Take A Giant Step

On December 1, 1955, Rosa Parks took a giant step. The law in her city said that blacks had to sit in the rear of public buses. Rosa, a black woman, refused to obey this unjust law. Her courage inspired many people—black and white—who began to fight for the rights of blacks. Try these writing ideas to honor her spirit and the spirit of others who take giant steps.

What Makes a Hero?

In no more than 25 words, write a definition of what you think makes a hero. Compare your definition with a classmate's.

What's in a Name?

Choose someone you respect and admire. Write a poem and begin each line with a letter of the person's name. Here's one about Rosa:

Remember her act
Of courage.
She made the world
A better place for all.

Team Time

Work with a friend to choose someone who has made a contribution to your school or community. Dream up an award to give that person. Write a letter telling the person about your award.

Bill Of Rights Day

On this date in 1791, the Bill of Rights, the first ten amendments to the U. S. Constitution, became effective upon ratification by the state of Virginia. Have students research why it was necessary to pass these amendments so soon after the creation of the Constitution. Why are they called the Bill of Rights? What rights do they guarantee? What states would not ratify the Constitution until Congress agreed to these amendments?

Rights For Children

In honor of Human Rights Day on December 10, try this class activity that will provide an opportunity for students to explore the concept of human rights. Begin by explaining that in 1948, the United Nations made its Universal Declaration of Human Rights. If possible, find a copy of the declaration and read it aloud to the class. After a discussion of why human rights are so important, have the class work together to create a list of Children's Rights based on the original declaration.   DEBRA MARTIN

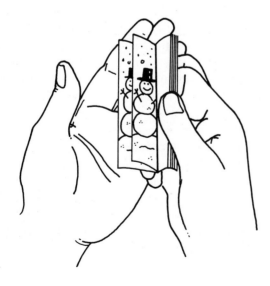

Cartoon Capers

Walt Disney, master of animated cartoons, was born on December 5, 1901. In honor of his birthday, have students make their own animated pictures with holiday themes. Give each child a stack of small file cards. Then show them how to draw the same character or object in different continuous positions—one on each card. When students have finished the drawings, have them put the cards in order and flip through them, watching the resulting animation. Students can hole-punch the left side of each card and tie them together with ribbon for unique holiday gifts.   MAUREEN CONNORS

Dazzling December

December glimmers and glistens with signs of the season. Dabble in some December dazzle—write now!

Holiday Daze

Choose a December holiday and write a poem describing it. Write the name of the holiday vertically on a piece of paper. Begin each line of the poem with a word that starts with the letter on that line. Use words that tell how the holiday looks, smells, sounds, tastes, and feels.

Winter Music

Choose a December holiday song or another song you know well. Write new words to it—celebrating the month of December or the season of winter.

Team Time

With a partner, go to the library and find interesting facts about dazzling December. Create a list of questions like this: "The man who created Mickey Mouse was born on December 5, 1901. What was his name?" (Walt Disney) Challenge other teams to answer your December questions.

Into The Wild Blue Yonder

On December 17, 1903, in Kitty Hawk, North Carolina, Wilbur and Orville Wright made the first successful airplane flights ever! Their achievement signaled the start of a whole new world of fast and efficient transportation. Let your ideas soar as you try these high-flying writing ideas.

Dear Wilbur and Orville....

Imagine you can send a letter back in time. Write to the Wright brothers and tell them about a form of transportation that they wouldn't know about. Possibilities include a helicopter, a nuclear-powered submarine, an Indy 500 race car, and a space shuttle.

Does it Dip, Skip, Soar, or More?

Imagine a new form of transportation and explain how it works. Choose a name for your invention that describes it. For example, *submarine* is made up of *sub* meaning "under" and *marine* meaning "the sea." Draw a picture of your invention too.

Team Time

Conduct a transportation poll with a friend. First, write out a list of questions: *What form of transportation do you use most? Which do you like most?* Then ask friends and family members to answer your questions. Write up the results and share with the class.

Math Marvels

The holidays provide children with many opportunities for mathematics fun. Here are a few ideas:

● Try a class project called Make a Thousand. Using needles with rounded points and working in pairs, have children thread cranberries into strings of 100 berries. Insert colorful designs made from construction paper after every tenth berry, making it easy for children to conceptualize 100 as ten groups of 10. Tie the strings from end to end and hang this larger-than-life decoration over the chalkboard, around the room, or on the wall in the shape of a Christmas tree.

● To stress estimation and multiplication skills, have kids work in small groups to estimate the number of kernels on an ear of corn. Give each group a calculator, then, one by one, have groups report their methods of estimation to the class. Some groups will make wild guesses; others will count the number of kernels in a row and the number of rows, then use their calculators to make accurate guesses. If ears of Indian (colored) corn are used, have primary-grade children estimate how many kernels are red, yellow, or blue.

● Reinforce the study of geometric shapes and symmetry by having children make paper snowflake designs. First, let students examine pictures of snowflakes to recognize their hexagonal shape. Kids can make their own snowflakes by folding sheets of paper to produce three lines of symmetry. For young children, you may wish to duplicate sheets that show fold lines. Older children may locate the fold lines by using a protractor or a compass. Tape finished snowflakes to classroom windows or use them to make mobiles or greeting cards.

● To reinforce estimation, addition, and subtraction skills, have children guess how many peanuts are in a large jar, then write their estimates on slips of paper. Distribute the peanuts among small groups of children and have them count them into piles of tens and hundreds. Ask groups to total their peanuts, then report their totals to the class. Kids can then add each group's total, and find the difference between their individual estimations and the actual total.   HILDE HOWDEN

Seasonal Envelopes

Here's a fun way to teach the skill of addressing envelopes this holiday season. Buy a package of greeting cards and separate the envelopes from the cards. During the first week of December, take the envelopes to school and give one to each child in your class. Have students address the blank envelopes to themselves. Check students' work for spelling and accuracy, then collect the envelopes without telling students what you will be doing with them. Later, sign the cards and pop them into the mailbox. (As an alternative, leave the cards on students' desks to greet them on the last day before vacation.) Kids will be excited to receive a holiday card from their teacher!   CARLYN HOVE ROEDELL

Creative Characters

Here's a holiday project to encourage independent reading and boost critical thinking skills.

First, choose a story with a holiday theme to read aloud to your class. Ask children to summarize the story's main ideas and write character sketches about the story's various characters. Afterwards, have children write holiday cards to each character, personalizing their cards with details from the story. Collect the cards and arrange them on the bulletin board, or hang them across the room on a long piece of string.   SHARON D. CHROPUVKA

December

Figure Eights With Skates

Here's a bulletin board that reinforces math facts for the eight multiplication table. First, cover the bulletin board with blue butcher paper and trim with a rick-rack border. Add a large, construction-paper cutout of an ice skater surrounded by cutout ice skates. Print a different factor of eight on each skate. Add ribbon laces for a finishing touch.
LONDA CAMPBELL

Winter Weather

This is the month to explore winter and learning. Adapt these winter activities to your own climate and grade level. Find out about winter activities in your area—winter carnivals, places to ski or ice skate, hiking trails, flower shows, and so on. Perhaps you can take a field trip to one of them. If not, pass on the information to parents for use in planning family outings.

Language Arts/Social Studies

● Ask kids to imagine what winter is like in another climate. If you live in a cold place: Can others go swimming in January? Is there more rain in warm places when it's snowing in others? Do different kinds of plants and flowers grow in warm areas?

If you live in a warm place: How would it feel to have to put on many layers of clothing to stay warm? How does snow feel and look? Does it have a smell? Discuss the differences between your winter and summer and how these differences affect life-styles. Do people go outdoors more? Are certain sports and activities more popular?

● A snow walk can help children identify some advantages and disadvantages of living with snow. Make a comparative chart, with students contributing ideas about how snow positively and negatively affects them—it's fun to sculpt and play with, but it makes kids wet, is cold, and makes walking difficult.

● During the course of a week or so, send children outside for a snow lab experiment. Is the snow the same or different from the day before? In what way? What could have caused the change? Challenge observers to use adjectives—*crunchy, smooth, powdery*—to describe the snow. If your climate is warm, ask kids to observe the sky over a period of time. Does the sky change? How do the clouds look—*thin, fluffy, dark?*

After listening to weather reports, ask children to write or dictate their own reports to describe the weather in your area.

Math/Science

● Turn the confusion of 30 pairs of mittens or gloves into a math lesson. After discussing the differences between gloves and mittens, ask younger children to indicate on a graph which type they wear to school. If you're in a warmer climate, substitute something familiar like different kinds of footwear. Older children ready for counting by twos can separately count pairs of mittens and gloves—or pairs of sneakers, sandals, and shoes—then report the grand total. Ask which set has more and which has less.

Introduce or reinforce the concept of one-to-one correspondence by asking students to match gloves, mittens, or footwear to their owners.

● Hold a "melt-off" to reinforce the terms and concepts *longer, shorter, more,* and *less.* Ask children to place ice cubes in cups or trays in various parts of the room: near the heater, door, and sink, high on a shelf, and on the floor. Record students' predictions for a discussion later on. Which cubes took longer to melt? Which took less time? Graph the results. What does the graph show about melting conditions? Why didn't the cubes take the same amount of time to melt?

● What happens to water when it freezes? Cut off the top of a paper milk carton and fill the carton completely with water. Place the carton outside overnight or in a freezer. Ask children to examine what happens to the level of water once it turns to ice. Explain that water is the only substance that expands instead of contracts when it freezes.
VALERIE BANG-JENSEN

December

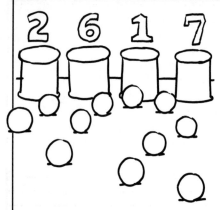

Snowball Math

Use this indoor game to practice multiplication facts. To play, line up 10 coffee cans—each labeled with a numeral from zero to nine—randomly against a wall. From a distance of three feet, a child tosses Styrofoam snowballs until two drop into cans. Kids score by multiplying the numbers. After two turns each, kids total scores.

VERNA SCHMIDT

Happy Bird Day

Help students identify local birds and record seasonal changes in bird populations. Ask kids to cut photos from magazines or to trace pictures of birds common to your area in wintertime. Tack pictures around a construction-paper tree. As kids sight a bird, they locate the corresponding picture and post it in the tree.   ANN SILFEO

Birds, Birds, Birds

Each December the Audubon Society organizes a Christmas bird count. The purpose of the count is to learn more about the number of winter birds and their habits. Keep your eye on the birdie with these writing activities.

Bird Watch!

Keep a birdwatcher's log for several days. Record where and when you see a bird. Include a complete description of the bird. Consult a bird book to learn the name of each bird you spot. Write a paragraph summarizing what you learned about the winter birds in your area.

Feathered Representatives

Find out the name of your state bird. Learn all you can about it. Then write a paragraph telling why you think the bird is or is not a good symbol for your state. If you think it is not a good symbol, tell which bird you think would be a good symbol and why.

Team Time

Work with a partner to create a mini museum of natural history. Draw or construct models of several birds that are native to your area. Display your birds in class with a written description of each bird and its habits.

Snowflakes Up Close

If you live in a frosty clime, this is one science activity that your class will call "cool." When kids take a close-up look at real snowflakes, an exciting project becomes a way to help sharpen observation skills.

To capture snowflakes, you'll first need to prepare materials. Place several glass microscope slides in a flat plastic container, cover, and put in the freezer. Also freeze a can of clear acrylic spray coating (available at hobby shops and hardware stores). When it snows, spray a thin coat of acrylic on the slides to hold the flakes. Catch some snow on the slides, cover the container, and allow to stand outside for an hour. Bring the container inside, then ask kids to examine their snowflakes under a microscope or hand lens.

BEVERLY MAFFEI

December

Hanukkah

Known as the Festival of Lights, this eight-day Jewish holiday commemorates the rededication of the Temple in Jerusalem. Hanukkah begins on the Hebrew calendar date of Kislev 25, 5751. Celebrate by sharing Aileen Fisher's lovely book of Hanukkah poems, *My First Hanukkah Book* (Children's Press, 1985), and for younger readers, Miriam Chaikin's *Light Another Candle: The Story and Meaning of Hanukkah* (Houghton Mifflin, 1981). Happy Hanukkah!

Sensory Writing Projects

Ask students to write about how they will use their senses during the holidays. Students divide their papers into five vertical columns and label each column with one of the five following category headings: hear, taste, see, smell, feel. Under each heading, students list five or more ways they expect to use each sense during the holidays, such as taste cookies, smell spices, hear music, etc.

JULIE STEMPINSKI

Holiday Time

December is bursting with holidays. There is the Jewish feast of Hanukkah. Christmas is December 25. Kwanzaa, celebrated by many black American families, begins December 26. Get in the holiday spirit with these festive writing activities.

Send the Very Best

Make your own holiday cards. Decorate them with the symbols of the holiday you celebrate. Write personal messages for each person on your greeting card list.

Peace on Earth and in Outer Space!

Imagine you have a pen pal who has never visited Earth. Write a letter to your pal describing a holiday you celebrate. Tell abut special family traditions and the personal meaning of the holiday.

Team Time

Work with a partner and decide what gift you would like to give the world! Draw a picture of the gift and write a note to the world explaining why it's important.

The Write Stuff

A parent/child writing workshop with a holiday theme is a good way to get kids fired up about writing and involve families in the learning process. Below are some examples of holiday writing activities you might want to try.

1. Have parent/child teams brainstorm holiday rhyming words. Then have each team use the words to create an original greeting card.

2. Give each team several sheets of construction paper and have them use the paper to create holiday placemats for the family dinner. Teams can write short holiday stories, poems, songs, riddles, etc. on their placemats for guests to enjoy at the table.

3. For a timed activity that stretches students' vocabularies, have teams write down as many holiday words as they can think of within a three-minute period.

4. Ask teams to list all the adjectives they can think of to describe a candle, a dreidel, an evergreen tree, and so on. End the workshop by presenting each participant with a "writing stocking" stuffed with colored pencils, paper, marking pens, crayons, cards, etc. Both young and adult writers will be equally amazed to have discovered that writing can be fun.

PAT GOLDYS

December

Christmas

Christians celebrate the birth of Jesus Christ today. Here's a writing activity from Kathleen Thompson called "Santa's Dilemma" to get kids into the holiday spirit: Poor Santa! His reindeer are sick. Even worse, a new species of cold-climate termites ate his sleigh. He needs a new form of transportation for delivering gifts on Christmas Eve. Begin by brainstorming a list of possible solutions to Santa's dilemma, then have kids choose the most unusual or original idea and write essays describing it. Follow up by having kids draw pictures of Santa delivering toys.

Holiday Trees

Decorate your school or classroom with trees for the holidays. The custom of using trees for decorations at the holidays began in the first half of the 700s in Germany.

A school tree involves everyone in the school. Ask every teacher, aide, support person, and student in the school to draw an outline of his or her hand on red, green or white construction paper, cut out the outline, and write his or her name on it. Make a conical-shaped base for the tree by rolling a piece of sturdy cardboard. Stand upright. Staple or tape hand cutouts over the base. Place a star at the top and you have a holiday decoration that everyone helped make!

A class memory tree makes a nice decoration and is a great way to remember every student you taught. Prior to the holidays, have your class make an ornament from colored poster board or heavy construction paper. Students cut out pretty shapes and paste their school pictures on them. Using a hole punch, punch a hole through the ornament. Thread a colorful ribbon or piece of yarn through the hole.

A few weeks prior to the holidays, hang the ornaments of previous classes and the current class on an artificial tree. Include ornaments for aides and other staff members. What a perfect way to remember the children you have shared so much with over the years.

SAUNDRA HOOVER   RUTH WEISENFIELD

Ornamental Vocabulary

Try this combination holiday-art activity and grammar review. Ask each student to cut out a large tree from green construction paper. Prepare shape patterns of stars, bells, and balls. Give to kids to trace onto colored paper for their own supply of ornaments. Students then write one word on each shape—nouns on stars, verbs on bells, adjectives on balls—and glue ornaments to their trees.

ELLEN AUCHENPAUGH

December

The Holiday House That We Built

When my class built a miniature house last year, what started out as a simple project grew into one of sharing and cooperation—a true celebration of the spirit of the season. As kids traded ideas, their project grew and the miniature house became our holiday home.

Try building a holiday house with your class. You'll need two same-size, sturdy boxes—at least 18 inches by 18 inches; samples of linoleum, carpet and wallpaper; fabric remnants; and other decorative odds and ends.

Stack the boxes to form two floors. Cut away box flaps so that one side is open, then staple boxes together securely, and place on a sturdy table. Ask kids to form committees to design and finish the outside and to decorate the inside.

Help each committee decide what to tackle first, as one detail will often inspire another. The outside committee might start with the roof, the inside group might first decide the number of rooms. Then children can work on details, like shutters and shingles and wallpaper and furniture. My kids were so ambitious, they gave our house a working doorbell and a yard with a clothesline, fence, and mailbox!

SISTER GWEN FLORYANCE

Let's Party

Add a jolly touch to a class party with these whimsical holiday decorations. To make each placemat, you'll need a 12-by-18-inch sheet of oak tag, red and brown drawing paper, felt-tip markers, ribbon, and scissors. First, cut scalloped edges around the red paper and attach it to the center of the oak tag. Lay two strips of ribbon, one vertically and one horizontally, across the placemat. Glue down. Cut a gingerbread man from brown construction paper; draw on eyes, nose, mouth, and buttons. Print the child's name below the buttons. Paste the cutout to the center of the placemat, where the ribbons cross. Laminate. The goody bag is perfect for toting party favors, cards, and treats back home. Just add a cutout gingerbread man to the center of a decorated bag. Punch two holes through the top of the bag and slide gift yarn or ribbon through the holes. Personalize the goody bag and add jingle bells for a festive touch.

TRILLIS SHRADER

Join Hands For Joy

Every student in your class can lend a hand to this holiday bulletin board display. Have children trace and cut out their hand prints from green construction paper. Next, staple the hand cutouts together, forming wreath-like O's as in the picture above. Cut the remaining letters from red construction paper to spell out your season's greetings.

ROBERTA FIELDS

December _____

Name _____

The Gift Of Giving

'Tis the season for celebrations and gift giving! Because giving a gift to someone is special, it should take a lot of thought and planning. What would you give to each of the following people if you could give them anything at all? (Remember, it doesn't have to be bought in a store.)

WHAT WOULD YOU GIVE AND WHY?

1. **George Bush** _____

_____

2. **Barbara Bush** _____

_____

3. **Mikhail Gorbachev** _____

_____

4. **New Kids on the Block** _____

_____

5. **Nelson Mandela** _____

_____

6. **Michael Jordan** _____

_____

7. **Princess Diana of Wales** _____

_____

8. **Bart Simpson** _____

_____

9. **Your Parents** _____

_____

10. **Yourself** _____

_____

KATHY FAGGELLA

December

Holiday Mail

Cover a bulletin board with blue paper. Add white paper on the bottom and scatter white paper snowflakes across the blue background for a snowy scene. Cut a mailbox from construction paper and spread out cotton and add to the top of the mailbox for snow. Attach colorful envelopes to the board, stapling flaps open. Then write a holiday activity in sequence on the back of a greeting card. Cut the cards in strips with one sentence per strip, shuffle the strips and place in an envelope. Ask the students to put the strips in sequential order. If the sequence is correct, the greeting card will have been re-created.

ATLANTA AREA CENTER FOR TEACHERS

Classy Cards

Try this quick and easy torn-paper technique to create striking greeting cards. Gather the following materials: red, green, blue, black, and white construction paper; white typing paper; and glue.

First, choose a holiday motif for the card, such as a candle, tree, wreath, menorah, dreidel, winter scene, snowman, candy cane, and so on. Fold a sheet of construction paper in half, then tear small pieces of construction paper into the shapes needed for the chosen design and glue them onto the construction paper card. Next, fold a sheet of typing paper in half and insert it into the card. Secure with a few drops of glue. Add a personal holiday message inside. Happy holidays!

SISTER MARY ROSEEN

Gift Box Riddles

This holiday season, capitalize on your students' love of riddles to promote creative thinking and descriptive writing. Draw several gift boxes on a sheet of blank paper. Make sure the boxes are large enough to write on. Then make up a different riddle for each box, containing hints about what might be inside. For example, one riddle might read, "It is warm and furry. It likes to lick your hand and play. It has a cold nose. What is it?" Distribute the worksheets and have students guess the answers to the riddles. Or, leave the boxes blank and encourage children to make up their own riddles for classmates to solve. Encourage divergent thinking by having kids come up with riddles for outlandish presents like a cloud or the Leaning Tower of Pisa.

LINDA GOOD

Joy To The World

To create this holiday bulletin board, first cut basic tree, menorah, and kwanzaa candelabrum shapes from oak tag. Have children thoroughly cover their selected shapes with tempera paint, then "stamp" the painted side on a piece of plain, white construction paper. When the "printed" images dry, have kids decorate trees and create candle flames with colorful thumbprints of paint. Mount the finished designs on construction paper, and staple to the board.

NEWFIELD SCHOOL
KINDERGARTEN TEACHERS

January

○ March of Dimes Birth Defects Prevention Month
○ National Eye Health Care Month
○ National Hobby Month
○ National Oatmeal Month
○ National Soup Month

Movable Events

January or February—Chinese New Year, lunar new year beginning at sunset on day of second new moon following winter solstice

Third week—National Pizza Week

Third Monday—Martin Luther King, Jr. Day

Third Monday—National Clean-Off-Your-Desk Day, to get organized for the year

Fourth Sunday—Superbowl, to determine winner between the American Football League team and National Football League team

Red Letter Days

1. New Year's Day. Parades and football games at various bowls mark the events of this day. What team will you cheer for today?

2. Isaac Asimov, born in 1920, has written almost 200 books for young people and adults. Most of them are on science-fiction topics. Ask for one of his books at the library. You will enjoy reading it.

3. Joan Walsh Anglund, this favorite children's author, was born in 1926. See if you can borrow a copy of her tiny book, *A Friend Is Someone Who Likes You,* to read to a younger sister or brother.

4. Trivia Day. Here's a holiday for those who know all sorts of facts that are interesting but not too useful. What bits of trivia can you share with others today?

5. Alvin Ailey, born in 1931, was an American choreographer and director of the Alvin Ailey American Dance Theater. What is a choreographer?

6. Do you think fog "comes on little cat feet?" Carl Sandburg, born in 1878, did and he wrote a poem about it. Find a copy and read it aloud a few times. You will soon know it by heart.

7. Until 1784, the only way one could purchase seeds for planting was to collect them from the previous year's crops or to import them from Europe. But on this day in that year David Landreth organized a seed business so U.S. citizens could purchase their seeds in Philadelphia.

8. Elvis Presley, born in 1935, was a very popular rock singer, whose music is still revered. Where is his home? Do you know anyone who has visited it?

9. Dogs trained to guide the blind were taught at "The Seeing Eye" in Nashville, Tennessee. "The Seeing Eye" was incorporated on this day in 1929 as a not-for-profit association. The organization moved to Morristown, New Jersey in May, 1929, where it still is. Find out how seeing-eye dogs are trained.

10. Oil had been discovered in other states many years before, but the Spindletop oil strike, on this day in Texas in 1901, was a really big one. What is a "Christmas tree" on an oil field?

11. In 1878, a milkman in Brooklyn, New York delivered milk in glass bottles for the first time. How was milk delivered before that? Is milk delivered to homes in your area today? What kind of container is it in?

12. We can thank Charles Perrault, born in 1628, for some of our favorite fairy tales. For hundreds of years people had been telling "Sleeping Beauty," "Puss in Boots," and "Little Red Riding Hood," but Perrault finally wrote them down and published them in a book called *Tales of Mother Goose.* Reread one of these stories so you can tell it to a younger friend or relative.

13. Stephen Foster Memorial Day. This song writer died today in 1864, ill and penniless, even though many of the more than 200 songs (words and music) he wrote were very popular. His "Oh, Susanna," was a favorite of the people heading for the gold rush in California. Find the words and sing it with the class.

14. An American officer, Benedict Arnold, was born in 1741. During the Revolutionary War he deserted to the British. What do we mean when we say that someone is a "Benedict Arnold"?

15. Martin Luther King, Jr. born in 1928, was a great worker for the rights of blacks in this country. Find and read excerpts from some of the speeches he made, especially the section that begins, "I have a dream."

16. You will like to read "The Cremation of Sam McGee" or "The Shooting of Dan McGrew," two long story poems by Robert Service, born in 1874. In what part of the world is the setting for these poems?

17. The only man to sign the four documents important for the new nation, the United States, was Ben Franklin, born in 1706. Read about him.

18. The record for the largest snowfall in a 24-hour period goes to Silver Lake, Colorado, where 76 inches fell, in 1921. Do you have snow in your area? How much? Look at the weather column in your local newspaper to see the average snowfall for your area.

19. Robert E. Lee was considered the greatest Confederate general of the Civil War. Born in 1807, he almost didn't serve in that army. What other army might he have led?

20. This is Inauguration Day, if a president was elected last November. Since 1937, this is the day a president is inaugurated. What does *inauguration* mean?

21. National Hugging Day. Have you hugged a parent today? Or a special friend? Your pet?

22. The first postal route in this country began today in 1673. The monthly service was between New York City and Boston, Massachusetts. Imagine what it would be like to get mail once a month.

23. Today is National Handwriting Day. Take this opportunity to practice your handwriting.

24. What did John Sutter's employee accidentally discover when he was building a sawmill in California in 1848? Gold! Why are people excited about finding gold?

25. Corazon "Cory" Aquino, born in 1923, is president of the Philippines. Name at least one other country that has a woman as its head of state.

26. Australia Day. In 1788, the first boatloads of convicts from England landed in Australia. This was England's method of keeping their jails from overcrowding. Why were they sent to Australia?

27. Wolfgang Amadeus Mozart, one of the world's greatest musicians, was born in 1756. You may want to see the movie *Amadeus,* based on the life of this famous man.

28. Two events on this day are important for ocean life. The U.S. Coast Guard was formed in 1915; the Merchant Marine Academy opened in 1942. Read to find out about one of these units. Why is it important?

29. Sing "Happy Birthday" to Oprah Winfrey, born in 1954. What qualities do you think she possesses that make her so popular?

30. Today is Purple Cow Day, honoring Gelett Burgess, born in 1866. Find and learn this four-line verse, then write you own poem about something you'd rather see than be.

31. Jackie Robinson, born in 1919, was a very courageous person. Why? Because he had the courage to try to play major league baseball and became the first black person to be on a major league team. Why did this take courage?

Resolutions

Let students decorate the classroom with New Year's bells to ring in the new year and ring out the old! Each student cuts out two bells from two pieces of 8 1/2-by-11-inch colorful construction paper. Then, on the first bell, students list bad habits they would like to stop, using complete sentences. On the second bell, students list good habits they would like to start.

Students sign their names to both bells and hang them on a bulletin board or classroom wall to remind them of their resolutions.

ESTHER "GRANNY" PARSONS

Time To Start The New Year Right

Usher in the new year with an hourglass of resolutions. Use white construction paper to create a large hourglass. Have students write their New Year's resolutions on oak tag circles and tack them to the hourglass, as if they were grains of sand. You might also want children to draw or bring in pictures relating to their resolutions. At the end of the year, see how many students actually stuck to their good intentions!

PAULA MILLENDER GOINES

Resolution Sled

Trace a sled pattern on construction paper. Print a New Year's resolution on the top or on a runner. Cut out, decorate, fold runners down, and display as a fun reminder.

DORIS MEYER

I will pick-up my toys.

Goals!

As a class, come up with goals for the new year. Draw a "joggers road" extending around the room, using goals as guideposts. Encourage kids to choose at least three to work on.

LORETTA WELK JUNG

Lift Off For The New Year

Blast off into the new year with this eye-catching display! Roll and staple a piece of poster board into a tube shape for a rocket's body. Cut a point into top of tube. Cover with foil. Cut wings from poster board, cover with foil, and staple them to the rocket body. Roll two small pieces of poster board, cover them in foil and attach to the rounded end of the rocket for thrusters. Use cotton and red and gold foil for exhaust. Background construction paper stars have students' names on them. Use construction paper and foil for heading.

ATLANTA AREA CENTER FOR TEACHERS

Calendar Catchall

Cut a paper plate in half. Attach one half to a whole paper plate for a pocket. Decorate, then fasten a small calendar to the pocket. Add the child's photo, if possible, attach yarn, and hang.

BARBARA ELLIS

Our Wishes For The New Year

Wishes For The New Year

Make a large wishing well from butcher paper, and boy and girl figures from construction paper. Place figures next to the well on the board. Arrange them to look as though they are throwing pennies into the well. The pennies are cut from brown construction paper. Decorate the border with paper pennies. Have each student cut out a penny from brown construction paper. The pennies should be large enough to accommodate handwriting. Students write a wish they have for the new year on the penny. Glue a new, real penny on the construction paper penny and laminate. At the end of the year, give the children their laminated pennies as souvenirs.

JOYCE ANNE MUNN

Class Calendars

This year, instead of buying a new classroom calendar, why not have students make one themselves? Divide the class into 12 groups of two or three children each and assign a different month to each group. Give each group a large piece of paper or posterboard on which the bottom third is squared and numbered like a real calendar. Let students complete their calendars by illustrating the top two-thirds with appropriate pictures, symbols, verse, quotations, and so on. For older students, leave each month's calendar grid blank and have the kids properly place dates for the current year, make notations of important celebrations and events, and put the months in order to form the finished calendar.

PAMELA GREEN

First In Line

It's a brand-new year, a time to think about firsts! Grab a pen or pencil and try these writing activities!

First Things First

Make a list of phrases that have the word *first* in them. Here are some examples: first base, first love, first things first. Choose one of the phrases and use it as a title for a silly or serious short story. The main character in your story should be facing a problem related to a first in his or her life.

First for Me

What exciting firsts are you looking forward to this year? Will you play on your first baseball team? Will you welcome your first baby sister or brother? Make a list of firsts for yourself and write a sentence or two telling about each one.

Team Time

Work with a partner to make a list of "firsts" in history. For example, Sally Ride was the first female astronaut and George Washington was the first president. Write a news story about it.

Jumping January

January is jumping with fun. Join in with paper and pen!

Old and New

The old year is often pictured as a tired old man. The new year is often depicted as a young baby in diapers. Write a dialogue between Old Man and New Baby. Allow Old Man to talk about the good things that happened—in your town or school or personal life last year. Let New Baby talk about the good things you hope will happen in your town or school or personal life in the year ahead.

Dear Congress

Congress assembles every January 3. Be part of this year's assembly by thinking about an issue that is important to you. Maybe you feel something more should be done in the war on drugs or to improve the environment. Write to one of your representatives in Congress expressing your opinion.

Team Time

Work with a group to create a January museum in your classroom. Draw pictures and write explanations of important January events—past and present.

Chinese New Year

There are 12 animals in the Chinese cycle of years. Legend has it that people acquire the traits of the animal of their birth year. Starting in 1984 with the Year of the Rat, the progression runs: 1985—ox; 1986—tiger; 1987—rabbit; 1988—dragon; 1989—snake; 1990—horse; 1991—sheep; 1992—monkey; 1993—chicken; 1994—dog; 1995—pig. Just add or subtract a multiple of 12 to match other years with specific animals.

As an example, children born under the rabbit love comfort and calm. They are intelligent, intuitive, have wonderful memories, and make wise decisions. Kids can look up more information in *The Handbook of Chinese Horoscopes* by Theodora Lau (Harper and Row, 1980).

In preparation for the new year, people pay off old debts, and repaint and clean houses. They also try to greet the new year wearing all new items of clothing. Caution: If you decide to hold an honorary classroom clean out, do it prior to New Year's Day. The Chinese believe sweeping on that day may push all your good luck out the door.

Another idea for celebrating the Chinese New Year: Switch a tradition involving mandarin oranges. The mandarin orange symbolizes the family for the Chinese because it has many segments under one skin. It's a Chinese tradition for students to present two oranges to the teacher. Why not turn tradition around and share oranges—mandarin, if possible—with your class?

Yet another way to share New Year's wishes: Send greeting cards with pictures of coins, peach blossoms, dragons, and firecrackers to one and all. Your class might enjoy making their own to send to friends, family, and others throughout the school.
BEVERLY MCNEILLY

Suffix Dragon

Brighten your room for Chinese New Year with this bulletin board. Cut head and tail of dragon from gold construction paper and decorate with sequins and glitter. Cut red shapes from construction paper. Write on them grammar rules in black and suffixes in gold pen (found in craft stores). Connect the red shapes with pieces of gold or black paper. Make Chinese children figures from construction paper. Add background fireworks by cutting red and silver tinsel and stapling to the board in bunches.
JUDY NERBETSKI

Happy New Year!

For Chinese New Year your class can make paper dragons to swerve and weave about the room. Materials needed:
1. A strip (18 by 2 inches) of green construction paper for the body, accordion folded.
2. Two green circles about 2 1/2 inches in diameter for the head and tail.
3. A green "jaw" strip 5 1/2 by 2 inches, tapered at one end and folded in the center.
4. Slivers of red tissue for the "fire breathing" effect.
5. Narrow strips of orange and pink tissue paper to fasten to the tail.

Instruct the children to keep the jaw piece folded as they make jagged cuts for teeth. Paste jaw to head piece. Add facial features.

For younger children, omit the jaw piece and paste facial features directly onto the head.
VIOLET JOHNSON

January Jewels

January glitters with the birthdays of wonderful people. Get to know them better with these writing activities.

Quotable Ben

Ben Franklin—statesman, inventor, and writer—was born on January 17, 1706. He is famous for his quotations like these: "Lost time is new found again" and "The used key is always bright." Write several sentences telling what each of those quotations means to you. Then write a quotation of your own that tells a truth about time or hard work.

The "I" Point of View

Martin Luther King, Jr. was born on January 15, 1929. Learn all you can about this great American civil rights leader. Then pretend you're him. Write a paragraph using "I" to tell about Martin Luther King, Jr.'s greatest achievements.

Team Time

Work with a partner to create a birthday card for one of the many great people born in January. Make your card for Edgar Allen Poe, Alice Paul, Lucretia Mott, Ethel Merman, Daniel Webster, Peter Mark Roget, Robert E. Lee, Jerome Kern, Franklin Delano Roosevelt, or Jackie Robinson.

Life was grim, just a bit scary, but never never a bore.
So to you on this special day,
Happy Birthday
never more

Patriotic Puppets

In honor of Paul Revere's January 1 birthday, put on a puppet show based on the patriot's legendary gallop to warn of the British army's advance. Kids make puppets as follows: Use cotton or a yarn ball for the head. Cover with a pink flannel square tied loosely at the puppet's neck and sew on felt features. Use fabric scraps to fashion colonial garb, then attach to head with thread. Top with a tricorn hat.

SUSAN AND FRANCO PAGNUCCI

Password: Thesaurus

Introduce your students to this valuable reference book of synonyms, created by Peter Roget, whose birthday falls on the 18th of this month. Play a game of "Thesaurus Password."

Make up a word list using 10 samples from a basic sight vocabulary or primary reader—*talk, see, home.* Challenge students to find synonyms for the listed words using a thesaurus.

Then divide the class into two teams, two players each. While one player from each team covers his or her eyes, select one of the basic words as the mystery word and show it to the rest of the class. Partners from each team alternate turns giving their teammates synonym clues to the mystery word. When the word is guessed, partners change roles and play again using a new mystery word.

Name _____

Reading With Your Fingers

Imagine what it would be like if you had to read without using your eyes. Many blind people do it every day. They read with their fingers by using a system of raised dots that stand for letters and numbers. They feel the dots with their fingertips. This system is called Braille. Braille was invented by Louis Braille, who was born on January 4, 1809, in France. Look at the Braille alphabet. Use it to complete the activities below.

The Braille Alphabet

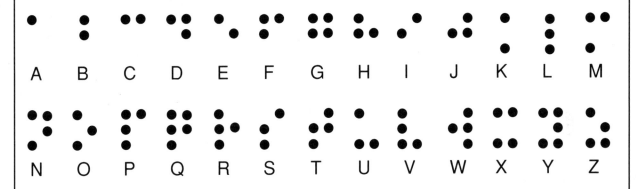

1. Find a message by writing the correct letter of the alphabet under each Braille symbol.

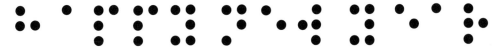

___ ___ ___ ___ ___ ___ ___ ___ ___ ___ ___

2. Write two of these upcoming February holiday names in Braille: Groundhog Day, Valentine's Day, President's Day.
3. Write a message in Braille to a friend. Give the message and the Braille alphabet to your friend. Explain how to decode the message.

Gold Star Ideas

★ The invention of Braille improved the lives of many blind people. Dream up your own invention that might help a handicapped person live a better life. Draw a picture of your invention and write a paragraph telling what it is and how it works.

★★ To get a copy of the Braille alphabet that your fingers can "read," send a note asking for the Braille Alphabet and Numeral Card to: American Foundation for the Blind, c/o Publications and Information Services, 15 West 16th St., New York, NY 10011. Include two 29¢ stamps.

Martin Luther King, Jr. Day

Born on January 15, 1929, and assassinated 39 years later, Dr. Martin Luther King, Jr.—one of our nation's most important and influential leaders—is officially remembered today. Explain to students that Dr. King protested against unjust laws and unequal treatment of black Americans. Black children could not attend the same schools as white children or enjoy the same rights and freedoms.

Pay tribute to Dr. King by reading aloud from his eloquent and moving "I Have a Dream" speech. Use this speech as a springboard to an art and creative writing project. After reading the speech, have kids create a class mural centered around the theme "Let Freedom Ring." What images will children use to represent freedom? What events or concepts will they choose to illustrate it? Have children work in small groups to share thoughts and ideas. Then distribute a variety of art materials and encourage kids to let their creative juices flow. Afterwards, have students write essays and poems that relate to King's speech. Begin by asking children to share their feelings about the speech in a class discussion. What does it mean to be free? How would children feel if they were deprived of their freedom? Post children's writing around the mural, in a hallway display, or on the bulletin board.

Understanding Race Prejudice

Most biographies of Martin Luther King, Jr., cite a familiar incident from his childhood: It was 1935 in Atlanta, Georgia. Martin, then six years old, went to play with his two best friends, brothers. The boys had always been playmates, but on this day, Martin was turned away. Martin was black and his friends were white, the boys' mother explained. Now that they were going to school—separate schools—it was best that they didn't play together. This event was a milestone in Dr. King's desire to fight racial prejudice. Help your students understand this important event with this activity.

Locate a description of the incident in a biography of Dr. King and read the passage to your students. Form groups of six students. Have students assume the roles of Martin, his friends, their mother, and Martin's parents. Have them write and share journal entries in reaction to the incident, considering question such as: How do you think Martin felt when he was told he could no longer play with his friends? How would you have felt? Has anything like this ever happened to you?

LISA CRAWLEY

A Great Leader

On the third Monday in January, we celebrate the birthday of Martin Luther King, Jr. He worked to make sure that all people could enjoy freedom. Think about King as you try these writing activities.

Words to Live By

Martin Luther King, Jr. believed deeply in these words from the Declaration of Independence: "We hold these truths to be self-evident; that all men are created equal." Write a paragraph telling what these words mean to you.

My Heroes

Martin Luther King, Jr. was inspired by Harriet Tubman, Frederick Douglass, Henry David Thoreau, Mahatma Gandhi and others who worked to assure the freedom and dignity of all people. List your heroes and why you admire them.

Team Time

Martin Luther King, Jr. believed in working peacefully to settle problems. With a partner, make a list of conflicts and some peaceful solutions.

Helping Hands

Martin Luther King, Jr. dreamed of helping other people. Celebrate Martin Luther King's birthday observance with this activity.

Discuss with the class King and his dream of helping people. Talk about how King didn't really know all of the people he wanted to help. Think about people who need help today. Discuss people in hospitals and homes for the elderly, as well as the poor and homeless in America and other countries.

Ask the class to brainstorm for ways to help these people. These could include bringing a puppy to a nursing home to share, or giving a play and donating the proceeds to charity.

Ask each student to choose a group of people he or she would like to help. Then ask the students to draw a large hand on a piece of tagboard. Students cut out the hand and write "I have a dream" on the pinkie. The child writes the group he or she wants to help on the ring finger. The child writes what he or she can do to help on the next two fingers, and his or her name on the thumb. Students then lightly color the hands with all of the skin colors of the world to symbolize all people working together.

Share your class' dream by hanging these "helping hands" in a prominent place in the school.

JILL BERENTSEN   ANGIE JOHNSON

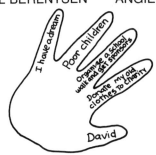

Dream T-Shirts

Dream T-shirts let kids wear their hopes for all to see. Don them to celebrate Martin Luther King, Jr. Day.

To make Dream T-shirts, ask children to each bring in a plain, cotton T-shirt. Remind kids that it was King's dream that all people be given the freedom to realize their dreams. Suggest students illustrate their own dreams on the front of their shirts. On the back, they can list steps they'll take to achieve their goals.

Two tips: Place sheets of cardboard inside the shirts to keep colors from bleeding through as children decorate. Try waterproof markers or acrylic paint and the dreams will be indelible.

BARBARA ELLIS

Name _____

Drum Major For Justice

The passage below is taken from a famous speech given by Dr. Martin Luther King, Jr. on February 4, 1968 in Atlanta, Georgia.

"I'd like somebody to mention that day that Martin Luther King, Jr. tried to give his life serving others. I'd like for somebody to say that day that Martin Luther King, Jr. tried to love somebody. I want you to be able to say that day that I did try to feed the hungry...clothe the naked...love and serve humanity. Yes, if you want to, say that I was a drum major. Say that I was a drum major for justice...for peace...for righteousness."

Copyright 1968 Estate of Martin Luther King, Jr.
Used by permission of Joan Daves.

More of Dr. King's speech "A Drum Major for Justice" can be found in
MARTIN LUTHER KING, JR. THE DREAM OF PEACEFUL
REVOLUTION *by Della Rowland (Silver Burdett Press, 1990)*

If you were giving a speech like Dr. King's, what would you say about how you would make the world a better place?

_____

_____

_____

_____

_____

_____

_____

_____

_____

_____

Put It In Writing!

Use your best penmanship for the following activities. Why? January 23 is National Handwriting Day. It honors the birthday of John Hancock. His signature is famous because he was the first to sign the Declaration of Independence and because when he signed it, he wrote his name in very large letters.

Big or Little?

John Hancock wrote his name in big letters to show King George he was not afraid. Imagine you are a signer of the Declaration. Would you write your name in big or little letters? What would you be thinking as you signed? Write several sentences explaining your thoughts.

Letter to a Letter

Imagine that the letters of the alphabet have personalities. What might they say to one another? For example, perhaps *q* is tired of having *u* follow it everywhere! Write a long letter or a short note from one letter to another.

Team Time

The name *John Hancock* is listed in the dictionary as a noun meaning "an autographed signature." Many other words come from people's names—such as *braille, pasteurize,* and *magnolia.* Work in a group to find as many of these words as you can, then compile them into a minidictionary.

Happy Birthday, Mozart

On January 27, listen to a recording of *The Magic Flute* and celebrate the birthday of Wolfgang Amadeus Mozart. This musical genius began his career as a composer at the age of five! While listening to a sample of his work, have students tell or write about how the music makes them feel.

Pooh Day

Christopher Robin, Winnie the Pooh, Eyore, and Roo: Where would we be without Alan Alexander Milne, the creator of these classic characters? This British author was born on January 18, 1882. Ask pupils to imagine that a favorite toy of theirs came alive. Would their new friend get them into trouble or would it save them from trouble? Ask them to write about their adventures.

On The Ball

January is football bowl month. Both college and professional football teams play exciting championship games. Score some points of your own with these sporting activities.

Ready! Set! Write!

Be a sportswriter. Watch a football game, or another kind of sporting event, on TV or on the school playground. Then write a short description of the game. Include the names of the teams or of the players, the most exciting moments in the game, and the final score.

Be a Sport!

Write five rules of good sportsmanship for *players* of any sport. Then write five rules of good behavior for *spectators* of any sport.

Team Time

Work with a buddy to create your own sport. Think about whether it should be a team sport, how points are scored, what equipment is needed, and other rules. Exchange what you've written with other teams and try to play their game.

Super Bowl Fever

Even young students get football fever. Try some of these curriculum-based ideas to help your class gear up for the Super Bowl.

Language Arts

Ask students to write letters to their favorite players participating in the Super Bowl. Mail the letters and display the responses.

Math

Clip pictures of players from the newspaper and display. Assign math problems involving football players and their jersey numbers.

Social Studies

Have children research the city the superbowl is being held in and write a report about it.   DONNA HEDRICK

A New Game

The rules for a popular winter sport were first published on January 15, 1892. Created by James A. Naismuth, basketball is a good topic for some student research. Suggest pupils use the encyclopedia or sports section of the library to find out why the game was created, how it got its name, some of its famous players, and facts about a college or professional team near your community. Some pupils may like to follow college or professional team standings published each day in the newspaper.

Having Courage

Being the first to try something new and different often takes a lot of courage. Jackie Robinson, whose birthday is January 31, was the first black American to play in baseball's National League. His outstanding talent and determination won him a place in the Baseball Hall of Fame. Have students write about an experience when they faced a "first-time" problem. Did they devise a special trick to help them overcome their fears?

February

- ○ American Heart Month
- ○ Black History Month
- ○ Human Relations Month
- ○ National Cherry Month
- ○ National Children's Dental Health Month

Movable Events

January or February—Chinese New Year (Gung Hoy Fat Choy—Wishing you good fortune and happiness)

Second full week—Crime Prevention Week

Third Monday—President's Day

Third Week—Brotherhood-Sisterhood Week

Third Week—International Friendship Week

Week of Washington's Birthday—National Engineers Week

February or March—Purim, Jewish festival to celebrate delivery of Jews from Persia

Red Letter Days

1. Langston Hughes, born in 1902, was a well-known black poet. Read one of his poems.

2. Ground Hog Day. Read to find out about it.

3. Norman Rockwell, a popular American painter, was born in 1884. Ask your grandparents if they remember some of the covers he painted for the *Saturday Evening Post* during the 1930s and 1940s.

4. A young pilot, Charles Lindbergh, born in 1902, had a nickname. When he became the first person to fly the Atlantic Ocean alone, he became known as "Lucky Lindy." Tell why you think he had this name.

5. The baseball player, Hank Aaron, born in 1934, became famous when he broke a record. He hit his 715th home run in 1974 to break the record of a man born on February 6. Altogether Aaron hit 755 home runs during his amazing career. Look for a book about his life in your library.

6. Babe Ruth, born in 1895, made 714 baseball home runs during his career. Read about his amazing career.

7. Laura Ingalls Wilder was born on this day in 1867. She began writing the "Little House" books when she was 65 years old. What other older people do you know about who are still engaged in interesting activities?

8. Boy Scouts celebrate their birthday today. Boy Scouts of America was founded in 1910. Does anyone in the class belong to a scout group?

9. Although many schools taught courses on forestry, on this date in 1909, the first school to give scientific training in the care and preservation of shade trees was founded. Ask someone who works for a tree surgeon to explain how to care for and preserve trees in your community.

10. Samuel Plimsoll, born in 1824, was upset about the overloading of cargo ships. He worked to pass laws limiting how much could be put in ships. Research how he made ships safer.

11. Today is Inventors' Day in honor of Thomas Edison, born in 1847. Edison said that genius is 1% inspiration and 99% perspiration. What did he mean by this statement?

12. Abraham Lincoln, 16th president, was born on this day in 1809. Research his life and write a short play about it.

13. Grant Wood, an American primitive painter, was born in 1892. Ask your art teacher to show you some of his paintings.

14. Today you can thank G.W. Gale Ferris, born in 1859, for one of our best carnival and amusement park rides. It's named after him. What is it?

15. A father and his son, both with February birthdays, are famous for interesting designs. The father was Charles Tiffany, born on this day in 1812. He designed jewelry and opened a jewelry store that still bears his name. His son, Louis Tiffany, born on February 18, 1848, created intricate stained-glass windows, lamps, and other objects. See if you can find a picture of an object by one of them.

16. On this date in 1960, the submarine *Triton* left New London, Connecticut on a trip around the world. It returned on May 11. Find out how a submarine submerges and emerges.

17. The contralto singer, Marian Anderson, was born in 1902. Known throughout the world, she was said to have a voice that comes once in a century. What does that statement mean?

18. If you had been with Clyde W. Tombaugh on this day in 1930, you would have been very excited. Read in an encyclopedia to find out how Tombaugh discovered our fartherest planet, Pluto.

19. Nicolaus Copernicus, born in 1473, grew up to make some unpopular theories. Until his time, people believed that the earth stood still and that other heavenly bodies moved around it. Copernicus believed that the earth moved. Ask a science teacher to explain the Copernican Theory.

20. In 1872, the Metropolitan Museum of Art opened in New York City. You will like to read the book *From the Mixed-Up Files of Mrs. Basil E. Frankweiler,* the story of two children who explore and live for a time in this museum.

21. The Washington monument, built in honor of our first president, was dedicated in 1885. It is in the shape of a obelisk of ancient Egypt. What is an obelisk?

22. George Washington, our first president, born in 1732, was also known for other achievements.

Read to find out about his work as a surveyor, general, and farmer.

23. On this day in 1945, some brave U.S. marines finally reached the top of a mountain in Iwo Jima, an island in the Pacific Ocean, after a battle during World War II. As they raised the American flag there, a photographer took their picture and won a Pulitzer Prize for it. Look for the picture in an encyclopedia.

24. The first rocket to reach outer space was fired in 1949. This two-stage rocket was fired from White Sands Proving Grounds, New Mexico and reached an altitude of 250 miles. How does this compare with the distance of the moon from the earth?

25. Adelle Davis, an American nutritionist and author, was born in 1905. Her message was "You are what you eat." What does that statement mean?

26. Thank you, Levi Strauss, born in 1829, for a favorite piece of clothing. Called Levis 501s, they are still made today. We usually call them jeans. Read to find out why Strauss began to make them.

27. Henry Wadsworth Longfellow, born in 1807, was a writer of many kinds of poems. One of his long narrative poems called "The Song of Hiawatha," was very popular. This story of the life and exploits of a legendary Native American hero, sold a million copies during the author's lifetime. Find and read some lines from this interesting poem.

28. Vaslav Nijinsky, born 1890, was the most famous ballet dancer of his time. Read to find out about ballet dancing and the skill it takes to perform it.

29. Leap Year. Every four years an extra day is added to February to make our calendar year more nearly match the solar year. Find out how you can tell when there will be a leap year. When is the next one?

February

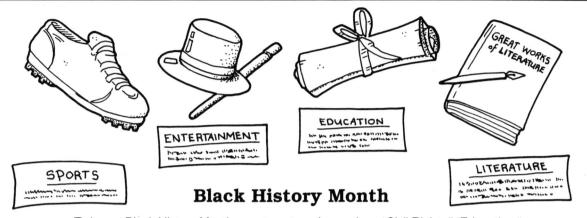

SPORTS

ENTERTAINMENT

EDUCATION

LITERATURE

GREAT WORKS of LITERATURE

Black History Month

To honor Black History Month, create categories such as "Civil Rights," "Education," "Literature," "Math and Science," "Sports," and "Entertainment" and use a specific symbol—a sneaker for Sports, a diploma scroll for Education, and so on—to represent each one on the bulletin board. Under each category place a caption on prominent black Americans in that field. For background information, see *Great Negroes Past and Present,* by Russell L. Adams (Afro-American Publishing Co., 1972), a collection of biographies of famous black Americans.

RHODA T. LONDON

Black History Collages

Make black history come alive with this bulletin board that reinforces social studies and art. First, have each child choose a famous black American, past or present, and pick several important aspects of the person's life to research. (For example, if a child chooses Ella Fitzgerald, he or she might do research on jazz.) Next, have kids make 9-by-12-inch collages using magazine picture cutouts to represent their chosen person. Place the collages on the bulletin board. Follow up by having students give brief oral presentations in character, then have them take turns interviewing each other.

CHARLAYNE MCLEOD

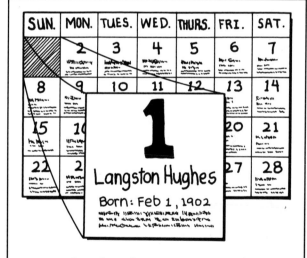

Black History Month

Construct your own calendar in honor of important black figures in American history. Names to highlight: Langston Hughes, Marcus Garvey, Rosa Parks, Benjamin Banneker, Martin Delaney, Paul Lawrence Dunbar, Leontyne Price, Absalom Jones, Frederick Douglass, Malcolm X, W.E.B. Du Bois, Hiram R. Revels, Marian Anderson, Phillis Wheatley. Kids research names, look up dates and interesting facts, and add important events.

VIRGINIA MEALY

JACK ROOSEVELT ROBINSON
BROOKLYN, N.L 1947 TO 1956

In Praise Of Black Americans

February is Black History Month. It's when we celebrate the black Americans who have helped make our country great. So pick up your paper and pen, and join in the jamboree.

Dream a Dream

Martin Luther King, Jr., minister and leader of the movement for black civil rights, wrote a famous speech in which he repeated the words "I have a dream." King's dream was a world free of hatred and prejudice. Write your own "I Have a Dream" speech. Tell about your hopes for the future. Deliver the speech to your class.

Who Am I?

Learn all you can about one famous black American from the past or present. Possibilities include: Harriet Tubman, Langston Hughes, Jackie Robinson, Jesse Jackson, Mary McLeod Bethune, or Maya Angelou. Pretend you are that person. Without mentioning your name, use the pronoun *I* to write a paragraph about your life. Share your paragraph with classmates. See if they can guess who you are.

Team Time

Work in a group to create a poster celebrating the contributions of one or more black Americans.

Black History Month

Pick up your pen and join in the celebration of Black History Month—a time we praise the achievements and contributions of great black Americans.

Words of Wisdom

Frederick Douglass was born a slave but escaped from slavery and overcame many hardships to become a respected author and speaker. He wrote: "If there is no struggle, there is no progress." Write a paragraph telling what you think those words mean and how they apply to your life.

Freedom Is...

Many brave black Americans have worked to guarantee the rights and freedom of their people. Write a rhymed or unrhymed poem that tells what freedom means to you. Start each new line with a letter in the word freedom. When your poem is complete, you will have spelled freedom down the left side.

Team Time

Work in a group to research the life of a famous black American. Then make a mural showing the important events in the person's life. Write several sentences under each scene to tell what is happening.

Lost Tooth Envelope

Losing a tooth can be an event, especially for young children. Add the following verse to the pattern illustrated here to create a supply of envelopes for delivering the prize safely home:

I had a little loose tooth,
When it wiggled it was sore.
But now it doesn't hurt,
'Cause I don't have it anymore!

When a child loses a tooth, place it inside an envelope, fold the flaps, seal with glue, and thread yarn through the hole. The child can wear the package around wrist or neck for the rest of the day.
JAYNE JOHNSON

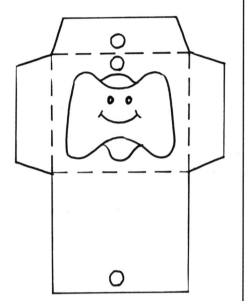

Tooth-Counting Contest

Try this simple classroom contest to prime your students for National Children's Dental Health Month. As a homework assignment, have each child count the exact number of teeth in his or her mouth, then print the tally on a small sheet of paper. The next day, collect the tallies and add them up, keeping the total a secret. Then, ask the kids to guess the total number of teeth for the entire class. Give a new toothbrush and package of dental floss to the student whose guess is closest to the total.
BETH LIVINGSTONE

Children's Dental Health Month

Sponsored by the American Dental Association, National Children's Dental Health Month is designed to increase awareness and stress the importance of regular dental care and hygiene. To send for a catalog that features classroom aids, write to the American Dental Association, Order Department, 211 East Chicago Avenue, Chicago, IL 60622; (800) 621-8099, ext. 2639. Be sure to contact your local dental association for more information on National Children's Dental Health Month events.

CHOMPER CHECKLIST
Brush twice a day.
Floss twice a day.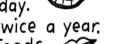
See your Dentist twice a year.
Eat healthy foods.
Stay away from sweets.

Chompers Checklist

It's National Children's Dental Health Month. Ask students to make a list of guidelines for healthy teeth. Tack these to a bulletin board. Invite the school nurse or local dentist to add suggestions. Kids cut out magazine pictures of white teeth and bright smiles, or draw their own, to create a border.
OLIVER HEREFORD

Name _____

Body Language

February is Dental Health Month. So take time to "brush up" on good habits for keeping your teeth in tiptop shape.

Did you know that teeth can be found not only in your mouth but also in what you say and write? For example, the commonly heard expression "cut your eyeteeth" means "learn something important" or "grow up."

Write the letter of each definition below on the line next to the correct body language phrase.

Body Language Phrases

___ **1.** by the skin of your teeth
4$$1

___ **2.** toe the line
13

___ **3.** tear your hair out
10

___ **4.** in the blink of an eye
56

___ **5.** have your head in the clouds
915

___ **6.** have butterflies in your stomach
12

___ **7.** pull the wool over someone's eyes
23

___ **8.** hands-down
14

___ **9.** get off on the wrong foot
11

___ **10.** keep at arm's length
78

Definitions

a. be nervous

b. lie to or trick someone

c. do what you're supposed to

d. quickly

e. keep at a distance

f. easy

g. just barely

h. start out badly

i. get upset

j. daydream

Tooth Quiz: How many deciduous teeth (baby teeth) and how many permanent teeth does a person have? Write the numbered letters above on the corresponding lines below to find the answers.

___ ___ ___ ___ ___ ___ deciduous teeth
123456

___ ___ ___ ___ ___ ___ ___ ___ ___ permanent teeth
789101112131415

Gold Star Ideas

★ Write down as many body language phrases as you can think of. Create a body language definition quiz like the one above. Give it to a friend to try.

★★ **Riddle:** What has teeth but never bites? **Answer:** A comb! Write riddles using a body part in the question or answer. Try your riddles on your classmates, family or friends.

Groundhog Day

February 2 is known as Groundhog Day, or Candelmas, as the early German settlers who began this tradition over a century ago called it. It is the day on which the groundhog, or woodchuck, comes out of hibernation to make a weather prediction. If the groundhog sees its shadow upon emerging from its den, legend has it that there will be six more weeks of winter. If the groundhog doesn't see its shadow, we can expect an early spring. The most famous of all groundhogs is Phil, who dwells in Pennsylvania and has been an "infallible prognosticator" of winter's end for more than a century.

Groundhog Gala

Greetings to the groundhog! Just look at how many different areas can be incorporated in lessons focusing on this furry friend.

Teach children new vocabulary words that have to do with this holiday, such as *groundhog, shadow, hibernate and prediction.* Go over these new words and talk about their meanings.

For a math activity, have children measure their shadows and compare sizes. Compare the changes that occur in the shadows during different times of the day.

For science, have children predict whether the groundhog will spot his shadow or not. Ask them when they notice their own shadows—is it when it is sunny or when it is cloudy outside? Talk about how the groundhog hibernates for the winter. Look up books on this creature and see what other fun facts can be found.

Have children draw their own groundhog. He can either be discovering his shadow or still snoozing way down deep in his comfy hole.

JERRIE ALLEN

Good Grief, Groundhog!
It's Groundhog Day (February 2)—but where is Phil?

It's Groundhog Day, and Phil, the world's most famous groundhog, is expected to make his long-awaited weather prediction. But poor Phil has the flu! His doctor told him to eat plenty of acorns and not to leave his cozy den. How can he predict the weather? Write a story about Phil's dilemma.

Fabulous February!

Celebrate fabulous February with these special writing activities.

A Word Picture

Make a list of February symbols, such as a *groundhog, Cupid, George Washington, Abraham Lincoln,* etc. Jot down a phrase connected with each symbol. For Lincoln you might write: "Government of the people, by the people and for the people." On a piece a paper, arrange the February words in a pleasing design. Add pictures.

Black History Month

Choose a black American who has made an important contribution to your city, state or to the country. Make an award certificate for this person. Include a paragraph telling why he or she was selected to receive it.

Team Time

Work with a partner to invent a new February holiday. Write a paragraph describing what the holiday is called, how it is celebrated, what special foods or decorations are part of the holiday, etc.

Happy Birthday, Boy Scouts!

The Boy Scouts of America was founded on February 8, 1910. Earn a merit badge of your own with these writing ideas.

My Motto

The motto of the Boy Scouts of America is "Be prepared." What do these words mean to you? Write a personal motto that sums up what you think is a good attitude toward life. If you wish, draw your own special crest, with pictures of your favorite things on it. Include your motto.

Earn a Merit Badge

Boy Scouts can earn merit badges in more than 100 subjects, including environmental science, emergency preparedness, etc. Choose a subject or skill you would like to learn or perfect. Write a paragraph describing the skill or subject and how you plan to learn more about it.

Team Time

Work with a partner to create a club, such as stamp collectors club or movie star fan club. Write a brochure about the club and its rules for new members.

Name_____

Be Prepared!

Your scout troop is on a weekend camping trip, staying in a cabin located two miles from the nearest dirt road. A major snowstorm is approaching and will continue for several days. You have enough provisions for only three days.

Your Troop Has:

a cabin with a fireplace
sleeping bags
food and water for three days
a first-aid kit
a flint kit and matches
firewood for three days

tools—jacknives, small hatchets, small saw
cooking utensils
clothing
a scout handbook
a radio

Think of several plans for survival or rescue. Then choose the best and tell how you'd carry it out.
KATHY FAGGELLA

_____
_____
_____
_____
_____
_____
_____
_____
_____
_____

International Friendship Week

A visit to a faraway place is something adults and children alike enjoy. One way students can travel to distant lands is to choose a country to read about and study. The country can be a place the student has always wanted to visit or the country of the student's ancestors.

Students may want to meet someone from the country they studied. One way to make new friends is to start a pen pal correspondence. Many groups and companies offer pen pal services for a nominal fee. These services will match students with pen pals of similar ages and interests in the country of their choice. Encourage students to write about their family traditions, hobbies, school activities, favorite foods, and vacation plans. When students receive a reply, have them read their letters aloud to the class.

Meeting and talking to someone from a foreign country is one of the best ways to learn about a different culture. Many communities have foreign exchange programs in their high schools. Sometimes foreign exchange students are available to give lectures and present slide shows on life in their home country. To find out if exchange students are available to talk to students in your area, contact AFS Intercultural Programs, 313 East 43rd Street, New York, NY 10017, or call (800) AFS-INFO.

Studying ancestry not only teaches kids about their heritage, but also gives them a sense of pride. Folklore, history, dress styles, political systems and religious practices can help kids glean valuable information about their heritage. Architectural styles and clothing can also reveal a lot about the geography, climate and economics of the country.

To expand this theme, have the kids design the traditional clothing of their ancestors. A family crest designed and researched by the students will complement the costume and can be displayed on a bulletin board. Or use these crests to brighten up a drab hallway.

Why not hold an international fair? Invite family members and friends to join the celebration. Have students prepare an international dish from the country they studied. Entertainment can be an ethnic dance or simple songs in a foreign language. And what better place to model the international costumes and family crests?

Inventor's Day Delights

February 11 is Inventor's Day in honor of the birthday of Thomas Alva Edison—one of America's greatest inventors. He invented the electric light and the phonograph and helped invent the movie camera and the telephone! Be inventive yourself with these writing ideas.

Ode to My VCR

What is your favorite invention that's just for fun? Do you think television is terrific or video games are great? Choose an invention that makes your heart sing and then write a poem about it. Try writing the words of the poem in the shape of the invention you're praising.

Crazy Creations

Over the years, inventors have created some wild and wacky inventions. One invention from the 1800s allowed a man to tip his hat by pressing a lever near his sleeve. That way, he didn't have to raise his hand to his hat! Concoct a crazy creation yourself. Draw a diagram of it, and write a paragraph describing what it does.

Team Time

"What twentieth-century invention has made the biggest impact on people's lives?" Work with a partner to take a poll asking people this question. Organize your results in a bar graph and report your findings to the class.

American Heart Month

The American Heart Association makes a variety of educational programs available to teachers to celebrate American Heart Month. Its "Save A Sweet Heart" program, for example, is a student-run, faculty-supervised anti-smoking campaign in which smokers—parents, teachers, and relatives—pledge not to smoke on Valentine's Day. For a guidebook on how to organize this program, as well as information on preventing heart disease, contact your local chapter of the American Heart Association.

Secret Valentines

Valentine's Day isn't just for students. Put the names of the staff on a piece of paper and have everyone draw a name for a "secret valentine."

"Secret valentines" exchange small, inexpensive thoughtful gifts each day (or as often as you wish to designate) until Valentine's Day. Leave the gifts in your "secret valentine's" mailbox or in a specially designated area.

Some gift ideas are: a decorated clothespin in the person's favorite color for clipping papers together, a scented candle, tiny bags or bottles of potpourri, learning center ideas, tea samples, stickers, old flash cards, posters, etc.

On Valentine's Day, reveal your identity to your secret pal at a special party. This idea can be used at any time of the year. ALICE N. RICE

Imaginary Valentine

Famous or familiar, there's a special someone each of us would love to get a valentine from. Who would kids most like to receive one from? Or to send one to? Ask kids to create the "imaginary" cards and then to share them in a display. Invite your principal, staff members, and other classes to join in the fun!

Heart To Heart

Celebrate Valentine's Day and American Heart Month with a heart theme for your February lessons for hearty learning!

Ask students to make a list of sayings using the word heart, such as "heart of gold," "heartthrob," etc. Discuss the difference between puns, proverbs and expressions. Students then classify the sayings according to these definitions.

Ask students to choose a saying and create a poem explaining what the saying means. Give students examples of different poetic forms to choose from, such as cinquains, couplets, haikus, limericks, etc.

Discuss the physical heart. Assign students to research the causes of heart problems and share the results of the research with the class, using visual aids.

Invite a physician to visit the class. Brainstorm for questions to ask before the visit, such as "What causes heart disease?" "What happens to the heart when someone has a heart attack?" "How do you treat heart attack patients?" "What can students begin to do now to prevent heart attacks?"

Ask students to create a monthly list of activities that affect the physical, spiritual and emotional heart, such as morning walks, mending a quarrel, visiting a lonely person or watching a rainbow until it fades.

MARY SCHROEDER

Keys To The Heart

This bulletin board matching activity works for reinforcing definitions of important vocabulary words in any subject area. Start by making one large construction-paper heart with a cut-out "keyhole" in the center. Then write the terms you want to reinforce on smaller cut-out hearts and place them inside the bigger heart. Write the definitions to the terms on cut-out "keys" and place them on the bulletin board around the big heart. Identify each term with a letter and each definition with a number. Students can then match them easily on paper. Include directions and an answer card to make the bulletin board self-checking. RHODA T. LONDON

Our Valentine Reading Worm

To promote silent reading in class this month, give children construction-paper hearts to tack on the board each time they complete a 15-minute reading session. Add pipe-cleaner legs and antennae, and include a colorful progress chart so children can see how many minutes they've read as a class. Have a Valentine's Day party to celebrate! MARY WILLIAMS

Be My Valen-Time!

Use your classroom wall clock to create this love-ly display. Mount the clock onto the center of a bulletin board, and fashion brown construction paper around it to resemble a grandfather clock. Surround the clock with ten smaller, heart-shaped "clocks." Have students number their papers 1 to 10 and ask them to fill in the correct "Valen-times." RHODA T. LONDON

All-Valentine's Day

Dress up regular subjects with valentine-related activities.

Phonics: Add a new twist to the party game of making new words using the letters in *valentine*. Ask kids to divide their papers into six sections—one for each word with long or short vowels *a, e,* and *i*. Kids spell shorter words, then place them in the correct sections. Remind children that each letter can appear in a word only the number of times it appears in *valentine*.

Writing: Ask kids to write and illustrate Valentine's Day stories inspired by these titles: "The Mysterious Valentine," "The Case of the Broken Heart," or "The Valentine Dog."

Spelling: Ask students to suggest words associated with Valentine's Day—*heart, red, cards, February, sweetheart*— to form a class spelling list. Words can be alphabetized, divided into syllables, and used in special holiday sentences.

Math: Use hearts to practice addition. Provide a heart pattern for kids to trace and cut out. Fold and reopen hearts. Now call out a number and ask students to color sets of small hearts on both sides of the fold that, when added, equal the given number. Then ask kids to refold their hearts, to write the total number of hearts on one side, and to complete the addition sentence on the other. SALLY STEMPINSKI

Name

Language Of The Heart

Riddle: What do squirrels give each other on Valentine's Day?

To find the answer to the riddle, write each "heart phrase" in the box on the lines after the correct definition.

HEART PHRASES	
a change of heart	heart-to-heart talk
chicken-hearted	be near one's heart
down-hearted	learn by heart
half-hearted	lose one's heart
heartburn	make one's heart leap

Definitions   Heart Phrases

1. without much enthusiasm ___ ___ ○ - ___ ___ ___ ___ ___

2. be fond of ___ ___ ___ ○ ___ ___ ' ___ ___ ○ ___

3. a new outlook ___ ___ ___ ○ ___ ___ ___ ___ ○ ___

4. an honest conversation ___ ___ ___ ___ - ___ ___ - ○ ___ ___ ___ ___

5. make one happy or excited ○ ___ ___ ___ ___ ' ___ ___ ___ ___ ___

6. afraid ___ ___ ___ ___ ○ ___ - ___ ___ ___ ___ ___

7. sad ___ ___ ○ - ___ ___ ___ ___ ___

8. indigestion ___ ___ ___ ___ ○ ___

9. memorize ___ ___ ___ ___ ___ ___ ○

10. fall in love ___ ○ ○ ___ ___ ___ ' ___ ___ ___ ___ ___

ADD IT UP: Write the circled letters on the lines for the answer to the riddle:

___ ___ ___ ___ ___ ___ - ___ - ___ ___ ___

Gold Star Ideas

★ Make your own valentine for that special someone. On the inside of the card, write a poem or greeting that uses a heart phrase.

★★ To learn more about the tradition of Valentine's Day, look for this book in the library: *St. Valentine's Day* by Clyde Robert Bulla (New York: Thomas Y. Crowell, 1965).

★★★Keep an "eye" on your heart by writing for a pamphlet on what you and your family can do to reduce the risk of heart disease. Send your name and address to: S. James Consumer Information Center, Pueblo, Colorado 81009. Ask for *Planning a Diet for a Healthy Heart.*

President's Day

Each February on President's Day, we honor all the United States presidents. This year, why not launch your unit on the presidents with some little-known facts about the men who helped make our country great? In *The Last Cow On The White House Lawn* by Barbara Seuling (Scholastic Inc.), you'll find dozens of offbeat facts about United States presidents. Use them to help your students realize that presidents are people too.   D.R. ANDERSEN

When The President Was A Child

Remind students that we honor our former United States presidents in February on President's Day. Ask each student to choose a former United States president and research his early life. Students should then write a paragraph telling about an interesting event from the president's boyhood. Allow students to read their paragraphs on President's Day.
          D.R. ANDERSEN

View From The White House

Ask students to imagine what it would be like to be the son or daughter of a United States president and to live in the White House. Have each child write a story or a diary entry about his or her life as the child of the chief executive.
          D.R. ANDERSEN

1600 Pennsylvania Avenue

Ask students to write a letter to the President. They may wish to ask him about his stand on certain issues or to wish him luck in his job.
          D.R. ANDERSEN

The Face Of The President

Ask students to think about what it takes for a person to get elected president of our country. Have them write a paragraph answering some of these questions: Which is more important—a candidate's ideas or looks? Why do you think so? Do voters trust a younger-looking or an older-looking candidate?   D.R. ANDERSEN

Hail To The Chief

President's Day honors George Washington, Abraham Lincoln and all those who have served as chief executive. Think about the presidents and their job with these writing activities.

Cast a Vote

If Washington and Lincoln were running for president today, which one would you vote for? Write a paragraph explaining your choice.

From the President's Desk

The President can write an executive order that has the force of law. President Lincoln did this when he wrote the Emancipation Proclamation, which declared freedom for slaves. Imagine you are president. Write an order for something you want to be national law.

Team Time

To be President of the United States, a person must 1.) be 35 years old; 2.) have lived in the U.S. for 14 years; and 3.) be a natural born citizen. Work in a group to list the personal qualities you think a president should have.

President's Day

Make President's Day more meaningful for students by trying some of the following activities about George Washington.

● Make a list on the board of everything students know about George Washington. Circle the characteristics students think made him a good leader. Review the list and make a new list including only the characteristics students think all good leaders should possess. Ask the class to define what makes a good leader, using the list to guide them. As you study other American leaders, ask students if those leaders fit the class' definition.

● Discuss what it might have been like to be George Washington's wife, older brother, friend, or stepchild.

● Collect stories about George Washington. Review the information to find out if the "facts" are correct. Discuss how people think of George Washington today compared to how people in his own time thought of him.

● Have students design a typical 18th century plantation or draw a map of Mount Vernon. Each building should be labeled or numbered (with a key) to indicate the activities that took place in each.

● Discuss Washington's feelings about slavery and compare them to Lincoln's. Talk about how people's beliefs change over time and how things people believe to be true as a child change over time, or how beliefs change as circumstances change. Discuss other examples, such as women's suffrage.

HISTORIC MOUNT VERNON: THE MOUNT VERNON LADIES' ASSOCIATION OF THE UNION

George Washington Hat Wig

You'll plan a George Washington play just to use this clever hat/wig combo. Use a neutral color 9-by-12 inch sheet of paper for the base. Make 4-inch diagonal slashes. Mold this piece over the head, overlapping edges, and staple into a skull cap shape.

Use a sheet of white paper to make hair. Draw a line two inches down from narrow end. Starting at a wide edge, draw lines an inch apart. Cut on lengthwise lines to make strips. Curl all strips in same direction over scissor blade or ruler. Make two sheets of "hair" for each hat. Staple to bottom edge of skull cap. Curls should be shorter in front, gradually longer in back.

Cut a 12-inch diameter circle from construction paper. Cut a 6-inch diameter circle from center. Fold edges up to give the circle a tri-corner look. Slide circle over skull cap till it rests on curls, with one of the points toward the front.

HELGA SHEPPARD

The Facts And Nothing But The Facts

Here's a presidential facts bulletin board in honor of President's Day. Ask students to read books about Washington, Lincoln, and other past U. S. presidents, then list a variety of facts about the presidents' lives on paper silhouettes. Mount the silhouettes on the bulletin board under the heading "Presidential Facts."

ROSE MURCEK

March

- ○ National Nutrition Month
- ○ National Peanut Month
- ○ Poetry Month
- ○ National Women's History Month
- ○ Red Cross Month
- ○ Youth Art Month

Movable Events

First week—National Volunteers of America Week
First week—Save Your Vision Week
Second week—Girl Scout Week
Third week—National Poison Prevention Week
About March 21—spring begins

About March 21—Earth Day
March or April—Passover, Jewish festival of freedom
March 22 to April 25—Easter
Last full week—Art Week

Red Letter Days

1. In 1872, Yellowstone National Park was created. Look up *national park* in the encyclopedia and find the one closest to you.

2. Did you ever hear a Who? Horton did, thanks to Dr. Seuss, born in 1904. Find a copy of *Horton Hears A Who* or some other book by this author and enjoy it all over again.

3. For years people had been singing "The Star Spangled Banner" and thinking of it as our national anthem. But it wasn't until 1931 that Congress actually adopted the bill, making it official. President Hoover signed it the same day. How many verses of this song do you know?

4. We can thank Jane Goodall, born in 1934, for much of what we know about the lives of chimpanzees. Read to find about the "tools" she observed them using.

5. Crispus Attucks Day. In 1770, this black member of a group of Boston patriots was the first person to die in the Boston Massacre. What was the Boston Massacre?

6. After holding out nearly two weeks, Texans fortified in the Alamo were killed this day in 1836 by the Mexican general Santa Ana. Read to find out why the Texans were fighting and what happened after that event.

7. Victor Farris, inventor, industrialist, and multimillionaire, died on this day in 1985. Of the 200 patents he owned, probably his best known one is for the paper milk carton. What is a patent?

8. Today is International Women's Day. What would be a good way to celebrate this day?

9. Richard Adams died on this day in 1988. During World War II when there was a shortage of paint brushes, Adams invented the paint roller. What simple device do you use that you would hate to do without?

10. Harriet Tubman, the leader of the Underground Railroad, died on this day in 1913. What was the Underground Railroad? What did she do to help more than 300 slaves?

11. The Great Blizzard of '88. It started to snow in the evening of March 11, 1888 in Northeastern United States. By the time it quit, 40 to 50 inches had fallen and winds had piled up drifts 30 to 40 feet high. What great rain, sleet, snow, or wind storm has hit your area lately? Describe it.

12. Charles Boycott, born in 1832, left his name to the English language. This real estate agent in Ireland was asked by tenants to reduce the rents because of crop failures. Instead he issued eviction notices. The tenants refused to have anything to do with him. Does this tell you what a boycott is? Define it in your own words.

13. One of the discoverers of "dephlogisticated air" was Joseph Priestley, born in 1733. What is the name used today for this air?

14. John Luther Jones, born in 1864, was a railroad engineer killed in a railroad wreck. His name would have been forgotten if a song had not been written about him and what he did to save the train passengers. Ask your music teacher if you can read the words to the song "Casey Jones," then explain his brave action.

15. The people of Hinckley, Ohio begin to look on this day for buzzards to arrive and begin to build their nests. What other places look for birds to arrive from their winter homes?

16. Jerry Lewis, born in 1926, is a comedian, actor, and director. But he is also remembered as the person who inspires the annual Labor Day telethon to raise money for muscular dystrophy. Find out about this disease and how it affect victims.

17. St. Patrick's Day. Find out why green is associated with this celebration.

18. Rudolph Diesel, born in 1858, was a German engineer and inventor of an engine that bears his name. What kinds of equipment are run by diesel engines?

19. When Congress passed the Standard Time Act in 1918, it established daylight saving time. When does daylight saving time begin today? When does it end?

20. And old television friend, Fred Rogers, was born in 1928. "Mister Rogers Neighborhood" has been a favorite television program for young children since 1965. When is the program on the air in your neighborhood?

21. Born in 1927, Cesar Chavez is a labor official who works for better conditions for Mexican-American farm workers in the Southwest. Find out more about the life of this serious man.

22. Marcel Marceau, born in 1923, is an actor who does pantomime. Find out how a mimist acts. Then practice performing a simple activity in mime. Present it to the class.

23. The first man to run a mile in less than four minutes was Roger Bannister, born in 1929. In 1954 he ran a mile in 3 minutes, 59.4 seconds. Look in a world almanac to find the world record now. Who has it? When did he reach it?

24. The first white man to explore the Grand Canyon from the bottom was geologist John Wesley Powell, born in 1834. What is a geologist?

25. The singer and songwriter Aretha Franklin, was born in 1942. Franklin has received Grammy awards for her rhythm and blues records and for her soul gospel performances. Read to find out what a Grammy award is and how it is awarded.

26. Do you know Sandra Day O'Connor, born in 1930? Sworn in as an associate judge of the U.S. Supreme Court on September 25, 1981, she is the first woman ever appointed to this high court. How is a person appointed to the Supreme Court?

27. Wilhelm Konrad Roentgen, born in 1845, was a German scientist who discovered the X ray. Read to find out some of the many ways that X rays are used today.

28. Johann Amos Comenius, born in 1592, was a Czech educator. His textbook was the first book in which the illustrations were as important as the text. Find a book in which pictures are as important as the text. Share it with the class.

29. The first car to exceed the speed of 200 miles an hour was a 1,000 horsepower vehicle driven on this day in 1927 on the beach at Daytona Beach, Florida. What other place in this country is often used for testing speeds of vehicles?

30. Vincent Van Gogh was born in 1853. Although Dutch, he painted most of his works in the countryside of France. His paintings bring millions of dollars when sold today, but he only sold one painting during his life time. We know much about his thoughts and ideas because he wrote long letters to his brother who kept them. Write a letter to a friend or relative telling how you feel about your day at school.

31. The first advertisement in a national magazine for an automobile appeared today in 1900 in the *Saturday Evening Post*. It featured the slogan, "Automobiles that give satisfaction." Create a slogan you think would be good to advertise a car today.

Munch! Crunch! Gobble! Slurp!

It's National Nutrition Month—a time to remember the importance of a healthful diet. So dig in to these writing activities.

Fabulous Fruits and Veggies

Are you a banana buff or a grape groupie? Do you think tomatoes are terrific or artichokes are awesome? Choose your favorite fruit or veggie—and then sell it! Write a radio advertisement persuading people to buy and eat more of your favorite fruit or vegetable. Read your ad with feeling—and sound effects, if required—to the class.

Riddles with a Bite

Why did the lettuce go to the psychologist? To have its head examined! What did the hungry percussionist do? Ate his drumsticks! What do you get when you cross a stoplight with a strawberry? A traffic jam! Write four food riddles—one for each food group. Try them out on your friends. Compile the riddles into a class book. Present it to the school or town library.

Team Time

Work in a group to design a poster encouraging your classmates to eat a balanced diet that includes foods from the four major groups. Create a catchy slogan and illustrate it. Then, write a three-minute public-service announcement explaining the importance of good nutrition and present it to your class.

Save Your Vision Week

Can you imagine not being able to see? Blindness can be prevented—over 90 percent of eye injuries that occur are avoidable. To get the message across to your students, stress eye protection during sports and eye safety rules during the week. Teach children the dangers of pointed objects, scissors, sticks, BB guns, and broken glass. Show them the correct way to handle potentially dangerous objects.

To drive home the message that sight is a precious gift, have students pair off for an experiment. One student in each pair will be blindfolded for a specified time period. The other student serves as a guide in case of trouble. But stress that the student who is blindfolded must do as much for himself or herself as possible. Halfway through the allotted time, have the students trade places. After the experiment, ask them to write or describe their experiences to the class. Did sightlessness hamper their activities on the playground? How did they feel in class, not being able to see the teacher's expressions or read the chalkboard? Was it difficult to maneuver in the lunchroom?

The American Optometric Association sponsors events in each state. Contact your state's office to see what events are scheduled in your area.

Sorting It Out

To get younger pupils geared up for National Nutrition Month, try this interactive bulletin-board activity that reinforces classification skills. Make a tagboard refrigerator with four shelves and label each shelf with the name of one of the four basic food groups. Tack it to the bulletin board. Then, use colored construction paper to draw and cut out several foods from each group and place them in a shoebox. Have children take turns reaching into the box, choosing a food, and placing it on the appropriate shelf on the refrigerator. Encourage students to classify foods in other ways, too. For example, have them put all carbohydrates on one shelf, fats on another, grains on yet another, and so on.

DOLORES MANGIONI

Idea Of The Month

March is National Women's History Month, and Newspaper in Education Week. A way to celebrate both events and review a history unit is to have students design and write their own newspaper based on a certain period in history. Use the same sections in the newspaper that are found in today's newspaper: feature articles, classified advertisements, editorials, sports, obituaries, and comics.

Then have students write a feature in the appropriate section about a woman or woman's issue in that time period. For example, an editorial about the women's suffrage movement could appear in the editorial page, with a feature about Elizabeth Blackwell in the health section, and a write-up about Babe Didrikson Zaharias in the sports section.

Students invent their own title and cost of the paper. They also illustrate their stories in the manner of the times (i.e., pen and ink sketches for the Civil War era, large illustrations for the 1940's and 50's) and invent advertisements that also reflect the times.

The format can be typed, handwritten, or composed on a computer.   J. STOLL

Classroom Women's Caucus

Let your students know that they needn't go back in time to find great women to recognize during Women's History Month. Many are right in front of their own eyes—in their communities and in their homes. To illustrate this, hold an informal lunchtime panel discussion that features prominent women from a variety of fields. For example, invite a local TV anchorwoman, doctor, teacher, attorney, letter carrier, or businesswoman to come and talk about her career. Encourage the children to ask questions. Afterwards, let them mingle with the guests over a brown-bag lunch. It's guaranteed to be an educational experience for all.   MILLICENT KOHL

Portraits In Needlework

Have your class pay tribute to women with a needlework arts project, such as needlepoint or making quilt patterns with paper.

Have students choose a woman in history and research her background.

Students use the information to create a quilt-block collage of the woman's life. Provide samples of different patterns of quilts. The local library, a needlework store, or quilting club are good sources of information. Ask students to glue photos or illustrations of the woman, her work, quotes, etc. to a piece of poster board in a quilt design. Pictures of the woman's pets, favorite color, invention or hometown can also be used as "quilt pieces."

The class posts each student's completed collage together to make a large "quilt." The completed "quilt" shows a spectrum of women and their achievements in history, and can be displayed as a wall hanging or bulletin board.

Students can also design and create a sampler depicting a particular woman in history. They design the sampler on a piece of graph paper. Demonstrate the stitches used in needlework. Allow the class time to practice the stitches on paper. Students draw the design with marker on a piece of burlap for the final sampler and stitch over the design using colorful yarn.

JO ANN MCALEER

Women In History

March is a time when we honor the women who have made both large and small contributions to our country's history. Join in the fun with the following writing ideas.

Here's Why She's So Terrific...

Imagine that you are selected to give a speech about a famous American woman who is being inducted into the National Women's Hall of Fame. Research a famous female historical figure. Then write a short speech telling why the woman you chose deserves to be nominated to the Hall of Fame.

History at Home

Talk to women family members and friends. Find out where they lived, what kinds of jobs they've held, etc. Write several paragraphs telling what you've learned about the history of women.

Team Time

Work with a group to create a mural called "Great Women in American History." Draw or paint an important moment from the life of each woman. Write a paragraph telling why the moments were important. Post the paragraphs under the appropriate scenes.

Great Women In History

Dear Madame

Research a woman from history whose accomplishments interest you. Then write a letter telling the woman what you admire most about her. Here are some possible subjects: Abigail Adams, Harriet Tubman, Susan B. Anthony, Susan La Flesche Picotte, Jane Addams, Emily Dickinson, Maria Mitchell, Deborah Sampson, Juliette Gordon Low, Sacajawea, Mary McLeod Bethune, and Phillis Wheatley.

Barbara Walters for President!

What woman living today would you like to see run for president? Design a campaign poster with a catchy slogan for your favorite female candidate.

Team Time

Work with a partner to create a book called *Women's Words*. Fill your book with quotations from famous women. Here's one for starters: "You gain strength, courage and confidence by every experience in which you really stop to look fear in the face...You must do the thing you think you cannot do." (Eleanor Roosevelt)

Name

Make A Little Music

The words of "The Star Spangled Banner" were written on September 14, 1814, by Francis Scott Key. Key was inspired to put his thoughts on paper when he saw the American flag still flying over Fort McHenry—the fort that protected the city of Baltimore—after a battle with the British. The poem was printed and soon people were singing the words to the melody of an old British song "To Anacreon in Heaven." It quickly became popular. A hundred and seventeen years later, on March 3, 1931, "The Star Spangled Banner" became the U.S. national anthem by law.

Celebrate this important musical moment in March by getting in a musical mood! Find and circle each of the musical words in the word search. Look for words across and down.

Gold Star Ideas

★ Many of the musical words in the word search have more than one meaning. Use a dictionary to find which of the musical words has the most meanings.

★★ Look in the library for these musical treats: *Young People's Concerts for Reading and Listening* by Leonard Bernstein, Simon and Schuster, New York, 1962; *The Star Spangled Banner* by Francis Scott Key, illustrated by Paul Galdone, Thomas Y. Crowell Company, New York, 1966.

```
T E N S M E L O D Y
E C H O R D A R B H
N O P P I T C H A A
O P E R A K E Y R R
R S C A L E N T T M
B T L N O T E H R O
A A E O R A O M E N
S F F L U L L A B Y
S F L A T T P E L R
B A R I T O N E E A
```

List of words for puzzle:

alto	pitch	harmony
melody	chord	staff
bar	rhythm	key
note	clef	tenor
baritone	scale	lullaby
opera	flat	treble
bass	soprano	

Bells Are Ringing

What happened on March 10, 1876, in Cambridge, Massachusetts? While attempting to perfect his latest invention—the telephone—Alexander Graham Bell made the world's first telephone call. Send your own messages with these writing activities.

Calling Long Distance

In the world's first telephone call, Alexander Graham Bell said to his assistant in the next room, "Mr. Watson, come here, I want you." Imagine that you could make a long-distance call to anyone in the world. Write a paragraph telling who you would call and what your message would be.

Picture This

Telephones for the future may have monitors so you can see the person to whom you're speaking. Write an advertisement that would make kids your age want to buy such a telephone.

Team Time

Work with a partner to write a skit about someone your age who makes a local call and gets a wrong number—somewhere in outer space!

Pop-Bottle Terrariums

Help kids welcome spring with this tried-and-true terrarium-making activity. For each terrarium, you'll need a two-liter pop-bottle, aluminum foil, potting soil, and several seeds or tiny plants.

To begin, cut the top off the plastic bottle and pull off the thick plastic bottom. Remove labels and rinse the bottle well. Line the thick plastic bottom with foil, making sure all holes are covered, and fill it three-fourths full with potting soil. Plant seeds (you can use dwarf varieties of flowers) or small houseplants. Water lightly until soil is well moistened. Add a ceramic animal, seashell, or pretty stone if you wish. Flip the bottle upside down and fit it into the thick plastic bottom section. Do not remove. There's no need to water the terrarium again.

To give as a gift, add a pretty bow or ribbon. Be sure kids protect the terrariums from the cold when taking them home.   DEBBIE MEINS

Spring Has Sprung

It's time to look forward to longer, warmer days and the retreat of Old Man Winter. Read poems that herald spring's arrival, host a kite-flying contest, or, if it's not too cold in your area, hold a ceremonial tree planting.

...And Goes Out Like A Lamb

Spring Lambs

To make this wonderfully wooly spring bulletin board, have each child draw a picture of a lamb, and color in the background any way he or she chooses. Glue on Styrofoam chips to give the lambs fleece. As a finishing touch, create a construction paper fence and add the words "Spring Lambs."   JUDY WETZEL

Float Away With A Good Book!

Here's an airy spring bulletin board that's sure to bring a breath of fresh air into the classroom. Cover the bulletin board with blue butcher paper. Add a large, colorful construction-paper hot-air balloon drifting under puffy white clouds. Have each child choose a favorite book and design a jacket for it. Then display the children's book selections under mini hot-air balloons.

RHODA T. LONDON

Sticky Games

On rainy days, use masking tape on the floor or carpet to designate lines for outdoor games such as hopscotch and four square. To make a large tic-tac-toe game, cut out "X's" and "O's" from construction paper, and let the fun begin!

REBECCA WEBSTER GRAVES

Foggy Day Fun

Here's a way to make foggy days brighter. Ask children to draw self-portraits with colored markers or crayons. Cover the drawings with white tissue paper to look like fog. To make the sun come out, lift the tissue. Read aloud the poem "Fog" by Carl Sandburg for added delight.

ELLEN JAVERNICK

Bursts Of Spring!

Let springtime bloom throughout your school. Print branches on construction paper using cardboard strips dipped in brown paint. Next, dip fingers into paint to print buds. Finish by gluing on small scraps of tissue paper for blossoms. Experiment—purples for lilacs, reds and pinks for cherries, yellow and white for forsythia.

GAIL NEU

Flyin' High

Kids post figures of themselves holding yarn and a kite. Next, children set goals and, as each goal is met, move their kites one space closer to the top.

MARILYN BURCH

Name _____

Create A Club

This month marks the birthday of the Girl Scouts of America. The original purpose of the group was to help girls become self-reliant by camping outdoors and participating in team sports.

Have you ever thought about forming your own club? Maybe you'd like to get together with other stamp collectors, pet owners, computer whizzes, music lovers, clown fanatics, chocolate-chip-cookie eaters, or...?

Complete the following create-a-club form. Remember: There's no "right" answer. Be as serious or silly as you like. _____

What is the purpose of your club? _____

Decide on a name, motto, and logo (symbol) for your club.

name _____

motto _____

logo _____

Draw your logo on the other side of this paper.

What are the membership requirements? Can anyone join or is it by invitation only?

Explain your decision. _____

_____

_____

Write three rules for your club.

1. _____

2. _____

3. _____

List three activities that members might participate in at club meetings.

1. _____

2. _____

3. _____

List three skills or qualities that a good president of your club should have.

1. _____

2. _____

3. _____

St. Patrick's Day Word Play

For a fun St. Patrick's Day activity, share this kooky quiz based on the word *green*. Ask students to name

- A song performed by Kermit the Frog ("It's Not Easy Being Green").
- A Danish island northeast of North America (Greenland).
- A retailer of fresh fruit and vegetables (greengrocer).
- What a person with a knack for growing things has (green thumb).
- A jealous ghoul (green-eyed monster).
- A worldwide environmental organization (Greenpeace).
- An expression used to describe a person who looks pale or sickly (green around the gills).
- Another word for money in the form of bills (greenbacks).
- A traffic light that signals permission to proceed (green light).

SHEILA KARR

Better Than Gold

Have students think of things worth more to them than gold. They could be such things as family life, honesty, or friends. Cut a pot for gold coins, a rainbow, some mushrooms, shamrocks, and a leprechaun for a St. Patrick's Day theme. Then cut several gold coins out of yellow construction paper. Have the students write their ideas on the gold coins with a black or gold pen, and paste them in the pot.

WAYNE SHUSTROM

Erin Go Braugh!

St. Patrick's Day is a day for everyone to celebrate—not just the Irish! Parades abound this day, with New York City's being the largest. It has been staged for more than 200 years. City officials in Chicago dump huge amounts of green dye into the Chicago River so it runs green on St. Patrick's Day.

People all over the U.S. and Ireland don green clothing to honor St. Patrick, a practice probably rooted in two Irish customs. The ancient Irish burned green leaves and boughs each spring to make the soil richer. The Irish also pinned a shamrock to their clothing to commemorate St. Patrick's death on March 17, 461 A.D.

Although St. Patrick's Day is an Irish holiday, St. Patrick was not Irish. Patrick was kidnapped as a teen by Irish pirates from Wales and taken to Ireland, where he was sold into slavery. He tended pigs for six years until he escaped to his home country, where he studied to be a priest. He returned to Ireland to convert the Irish pagans to Christianity, and worked as a missionary for 30 years.

The shamrock became associated with Patrick because he used it to illustrate the Christian idea of the Trinity, where the Father, Son, and Holy Spirit are one being. Patrick used the shamrock to symbolize the Trinity, noting the plant has three leaves, but still is one. Patrick became the second bishop of Ireland and is credited with bringing Christianity to Ireland, also known as "the Isle of Saints." He also is credited with many miracles, such as driving the snakes from Ireland and even raising the dead.

Americans borrow many customs from the Irish on St. Patrick's Day. What other holidays can students think of in which Americans have borrowed ancient customs?

Name _____

Hurray For The Irish And Everyone Else!

March 17 is St. Patrick's Day. It's a holiday that celebrates the patron saint of Ireland and all things Irish.

The word Irish is a proper adjective formed from the country name Ireland. In the box below are 12 proper adjectives. Write each proper adjective under the name of the country from which the word is formed.

Proper Adjectives

American	Chinese	German	Polish
Brazilian	Danish	Greek	Russian
Canadian	French	Irish	Vietnamese

1. Ireland

— — — — — —

2. America

— — — — — — — —
      2

3. Denmark

— — — — — —
      11

4. China

— — — — — — —
   3

5. Russia

— — — — — —
8

6. Canada

— — — — — — — —
  9

7. France

— — — — — —
      4

8. Poland

— — — — — —
      6

9. Germany

— — — — — —
10

10. Greece

— — — — —
5

11. Vietnam

— — — — — — — — — —
          1

12. Brazil

— — — — — — — —
7

Add it up

How do the Irish say "Ireland forever" in Gaelic, the ancient language of Ireland? Find this familiar St. Patrick's Day phrase by writing the numbered letters above on the corresponding lines below.

— — — —   — —   — — — — —
1   2   3   4   5   6   7   8   9   10   11

April

○ Cancer Control Month
○ Keep America Beautiful Month
○ Month of the Young Child
○ National Humor Month

Movable Events

First Friday the 13th of each year—Blame Someone Else Day
First Sunday—daylight savings time begins at 2:00 A.M.
Last week—National Library Week
Last week—Professional Secretaries Week

Red Letters Day

1. April Fool's Day. Find out how this day came to be.

2. International Children's Book Day is celebrated on the anniversary of the birth of Hans Christian Andersen, born in 1805. Read *The Ugly Duckling* or *The Emperor's New Clothes.*

3. What would it be like to lay down for a short nap and wake up 20 years later? That's what happened in a story by Washington Irving, born in 1783. Suppose that happened to you. Think about it, then tell what things would have changed, what things might have remained the same.

4. Maya Angelou, born in 1928, is a black author who has written many books for adults. Ask your librarian for her book *I Know Why The Caged Bird Sings.*

5. General Colin L. Powell was born in 1937. After graduating from college, this son of Jamaican immigrants entered military service. Today he is chairman of the Joint Chiefs of Staff. What qualities does a person in this position need?

6. Robert C. Peary, four Eskimos, and another American Matthew Henson, reached the North Pole on this day in 1909. Read about Peary's two previous failures and how he did not give up.

7. World Health Day. Name ways you can improve your health.

8. Many people were out of work in 1935. On this day, an emergency relief appropriation act was approved to provide employment to people who would carry out useful projects. The Works Progress Administration built streets, bridges, parks, and other projects. Bronze plaques are on many of the projects. Find one in your area.

9. At 1:30 P.M., in 1865, General Robert E. Lee surrendered his Confederate troops to General Ulysses S. Grant. Read to find out what Confederate soldiers and officers were allowed to keep as they left for their homes after the surrender.

10. The first Arbor Day was in 1872 in Nebraska. Today Arbor Day is celebrated at different times in different states. When is it observed where you live?

11. In 1938, 26 people gathered in Tulsa, Oklahoma and formed the SPEBSQSA. What do the letters stand for? Clue: barbershop quartet singing.

12. Anniversary of the Big Wind. In 1934, three weather observers at the Mt. Washington, New Hampshire Observatory, recorded the speed of wind. Gusts reached 231 miles per hour, the strongest natural wind ever recorded. Read your newspaper to see what the wind speed was in your town today.

13. Thomas Jefferson, born in 1743, was our third president of the United States. What is he remembered for?

14. Pan American Day. Twenty republics celebrate this day as a reminder of the independence of American nations and the cooperation they practice with one another. Who belongs to the Pan American Union?

15. Income Tax Day. This is the day when all federal and state income tax returns must be mailed. When did the U.S. first have an income tax? Does your state have an income tax?

16. Kareem Abdul-Jabbar, born in 1947, is a basketball superstar. Why is someone called a superstar? What other superstars can you name?

17. Surveyor III, a lunar probe vehicle, landed on the moon in 1967. Its digging apparatus told NASA what the moon's surface was like. Why was it important to know this?

18. The San Francisco Earthquake, in 1906, destroyed 10,000 acres and killed nearly 4,000 people. A second serious earthquake hit San Francisco on October 17, 1989. How much damage was done during this quake?

19. John Parker Day. This captain of the Minute Men told them to stand their ground at Lexington Green in Massachusetts in 1775. His order was, "...if they mean to have a war, let it begin here." Who were they? What did Parker mean?

20. Have you seen the statue of Abraham Lincoln in the Lincoln Memorial in Washington, D.C.? It was created by Daniel Chester French, born today in 1850. Find a picture of it. What other statues did the French create?

21. Sing "Happy Birthday" to Friedrich Froebel, born in 1782. He founded the kindergarten system in Germany. The first U.S. public school kindergarten opened in St. Louis in 1873. What did you like best about kindergarten?

22. The first Earth Day was held today in 1970. Today Earth Day is celebrated on the first day of spring. What did you do this year on Earth Day?

23. On this day in 1616, William Shakespeare died. Find the name of a play by Shakespeare and ask someone to tell you the plot.

24. Robert Penn Warren, born in 1905, was named Poet Laureate by the Librarian of Congress in 1986. What is a *poet laureate*?

25. Martin Waldseemuller was a geographer and mapmaker. On this day in 1507, he published a geography book and on a map of the world he called a newly discovered continent *America*. Where did he get that name?

26. John James Audubon, born in 1785, liked to sketch birds and their habitats. Read to find the purpose and work of a society named after him.

27. National Youth Workout Day. Today is the day when teachers and parents should work together to help you become more physically fit. What new kinds of exercises and activities will you undertake?

28. In 1939, Powel Crosley, Jr., produced a new car, called a Crosley. It was the first miniature car manufactured in the United States. It had two cylinders and a four-gallon gas tank. The two passenger model sold for $325; the four-passenger model cost $350. What does an average new car cost today?

29. The patent to the zipper was granted to Gideon Sundback in 1913. In 1932, the Goodrich Company named galoshes with slide fasteners "zippers" because of the sound the fasteners made. Using words that mean the sounds they make is called onomatopoeia. What other words do you know that use *onomatopoeia*?

30. The first president to appear on television was Franklin D. Roosevelt in 1939. He spoke at the opening of the New York World's Fair, at Flushing, N.Y. When was the last time you saw the president on television?

Child Abuse Prevention Month

National Child Abuse Prevention Month stresses the important roles of parents, teachers, and other concerned adults in the prevention of child abuse. For a free teaching packet and catalog, write to the National Committee for the Prevention of Child Abuse (NCPCA), P.O. Box 2866 IM, Chicago, IL 60690.

World Health Day

World Health Day is celebrated every April 7 to call attention to the importance of maintaining and improving good health and health conditions across the globe. The best way to start improving world health is to start right in your own neighborhood!

Encourage your class to participate in World Health Day activities by holding a health fair. Distribute information about weight loss, healthy diet, exercise, accident prevention and other health topics. Invite health professionals to speak to students about specific areas of interest, such as sports protection, stress, or careers in the health professions.

Demonstrations can be given on topics such as CPR and first aid. Races and other fun physical games can be held to promote physical fitness.

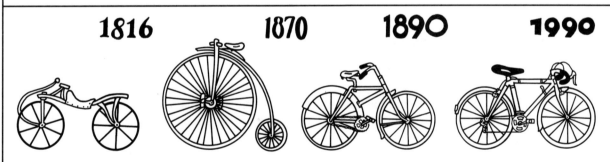

In The Good Ol' Bicycle Days

Bicycle Through History

In honor of Bicycle Safety Week make a wall-sized time line tracing the history of bicycles. Start with the French hobby-horse and work up to today's ten-speed bike. Here are some models and dates to include on your time line: *celerifere* (1791); *draisienne* (1816); dandy (1818); first pedal bike (1839); boneshaker (1864); ariel or ordinary (1870); tricycle (1871); safety bike (1885); sociable (1886); monocycle (1869); french giraffe (1890).

Kids can research each bicycle, illustrate it, and post their illustrations in the appropriate place on the time line. Ask kids to research developments in bicycle safety, too. What safety features have been added to bicycles over the years? Can kids think of additional safety features to include on modern bikes?

DOROTHY ZJAWIN

Sending Good Wishes

Today, it's easy for us to stay in touch with relatives and friends who live in faraway places. All we have to do is drop a letter into a mailbox or pick up the phone. It wasn't always so simple, though. This month is the anniversary of the Pony Express—a mail service on horseback! Think about how far we've come in the world of communications as you put pencil to paper.

Over the Rivers, Across the Plains

Most riders on the Pony Express rode about 75 miles at a time. One rider named F. X. Aubrey, however, rode for about 800 miles without stopping! It took him almost six days to go from Santa Fe, New Mexico, to Independence, Missouri. Imagine that you are that rider. Write a diary entry telling about what you saw, did, and felt during your long ride.

Let Your Brainwaves Do the Talking

Write a science-fiction story about a time in the future when a new machine can read people's minds. What funny or scary things might happen to a boy or girl your age who had one of these communication devices?

Team Time

Create a word-and-picture time line of the major developments in communication. You might include the alphabet, as well as the invention of paper, movable type, newspapers, telegraph, printing press, photograph, typewriter, telephone, phonograph, radio, television, computer, satellite, transistor, videotape, optical fiber, and videodisc. Present your time line to the class.

Week Of The Young Child

In honor of the Week of the Young Child, have pupils take time to think about what they were like when they were younger. Suggest they talk to members of their family about interesting events and episodes in their lives. Then have them write about and illustrate one of these times. Mount the finished pieces on a bulletin board entitled "When We Were Young."

Intro To Research Skills

Give your students a list of April events. Assign each student to do a research project about one event. Make a large calendar to hang on the bulletin board. Each student will draw a picture to illustrate his or her event in the appropriate spot for display when presenting his or her report. Display the finished reports on the board with the calendar.
GARY CHAMBERLAIN

April

Happy Birthday, John James Audubon!

John James Audubon was born April 26, 1785. Celebrate his birthday by asking children to choose a bird to draw. Back each beak with paper to form a pocket, then tack bird to bulletin board. Kids make up five questions about their birds and research the answers. They write each question on a card—with the answer on the back—and place it inside their bird's beak. Kids answer one another's questions.

RENATE WEHTJE

Keep America Beautiful Month

Celebrate Keep America Beautiful Month by encouraging your students to help put litter in its place to create a better, cleaner community. Keep America Beautiful, Inc., a nonprofit public education organization dedicated to improving waste-handling practices, has put together an interdisciplinary curriculum guide for grades K-6 called *Waste in Place.* The guide includes a complete teaching unit for each grade, plus a comprehensive bibliography and several resource materials lists. For a copy of *Waste in Place,* send a check or money order for $45 to Keep America Beautiful, Inc., 9 W. Broad St., Stamford, CT 06902.

Pumpkin Patch

Although it may sound premature, now's the time to get a jump on Halloween. In late spring or early summer, plant pumpkin seeds to grow pumpkins for each student in your class. If you start planting now, you'll have a whole crop of pumpkins by October—just in time for a class pumpkin-carving contest.

WENDY BINGER MORRIS

Earth Day Celebration

To celebrate Earth Day, try these quick activities designed to promote student awareness of environmental issues.

As a class project, have students collect paper, glass, aluminum, and plastic to take to the local recycling plant. Let students use the money they've collected from their contributions to buy a tree to plant on school grounds.

Form two teams and conduct a lively debate on the topic, "Human beings are earth's most intelligent animals." Ask who agrees and who disagrees—then let the debate begin!

Make a construction-paper food chain. Have children write the names of each member of the ecological community on strips of construction paper. Beginning with human beings, link the strips together in order of predation. Follow up by discussing what happens to the food chain when animals' habitats are destroyed by pollution or land development. Brainstorm ways in which animal habitats can be preserved.

MARY ANN BRENSEL

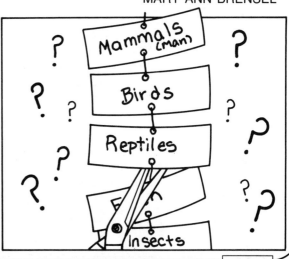

America The Beautiful

Put your pen or pencil to work and celebrate Keep America Beautiful Week—the third week in April.

Keep It Beautiful Because...

Think of a beautiful place in or near your town or city. It might be a lake or a park or even the street where you live. Write a letter to the editor of your local newspaper. Describe the place and tell why it is important to keep it beautiful.

Whodunit?

Write a short mystery story. Have the detective discover "Whodunit" by following a trail of litter that the criminal left behind. Have the criminal confess and express regret for committing the crime and for littering!

Team Time

Work in a group to create a poster to remind the kids at school not to litter. Make up a slogan like "Have a Bash—But Pick Up the Trash!" Then illustrate the slogan. Ask your teacher if you can display the poster.

America The Beautiful

April is Keep America Beautiful Month. It's also the time to observe National Wildlife Week. Some states celebrate Arbor Day on April 22 by planting new trees. Think about protecting and respecting the natural world around you with these writing ideas.

A Word from the Dodo

Create an environmental cartoon strip. Choose an animal that is now extinct as the main character. Possibilities include the dodo, the passenger pigeon, or the auk. Allow the character to spot and correct humans who are endangering animal or plant life. Make it as funny or as serious as you'd like.

I, America

Write a story, poem, or song in which America speaks using the pronoun *I*. Have America talk about its natural beauty, how it is being threatened, and why it is important for us all to do our part. Conclude your story, poem, or song by having America offer tips and suggestions for keeping America beautiful.

Team Time

Work in a group to research a wilderness area in your state. Design and create a travel brochure telling visitors about its unique features. If possible, work to organize a class trip there.

Arbor Day

Although Arbor Day falls on different days across the U.S. and in foreign countries, the first Arbor Day was held in Nebraska on April 22 in the late 1800s. It was then that a mass tree planting was held to protect the environment from wind and water erosion.

Trees are wonderful topics for poetry, art and activities. You don't have to live in the country; trees are there for children to observe in parks and school yards and to inspire them for the following activities.

Ask children to write a story about being a tree. What would it be like to live in a forest and hold your branches high all day? How would you feel if animals built nests in you, played on you, and wind and weather beat on you? What would you say or do?

Try this picture for writing poems. Place a large picture of a forest scene at the front of the classroom so every can see it. Ask the children to look at it closely and write a poem about it in a specified period of time.

What would it be like to be lost in a forest on another planet? What would the trees and animals look like there? How would they compare to those on Earth? Have students write a story describing their adventures.

Ask the class to make a list of every forest product they can. Give a few examples. After students read their lists aloud, read a list of forest products. Have students think of items they could substitute for forest products, or ways to recycle them. Recycling means reusing the item, not necessarily in its original form. Students can invent new uses for old items.

A popular activity around Arbor Day is adopting a tree. Children choose a tree in the school yard or park. They prune, water, fertilize and care for the tree as if it were their own. Have students keep a tree diary, noting its condition. Does it appear to be healthy? Are its branches straight and tall? Is it infested with insects or fungus? What types of animals make their homes in the tree? What seems to be the condition of the tree before and after it has been adopted. This type of activity encourages observation as well as good writing skills. DONALD A. VANNAN

Adopt A Tree

Have your students become partners with nature. Ask the class to choose a tree in the school yard or neighborhood to adopt in honor of Arbor Day. The students will study the tree, and along with nature, help it to thrive.

First, take the class on a walk around the school to look at possible candidates for adoption. Create a nominating committee and conduct a vote for the tree.

Once selected, the class may wish to label the tree temporarily to indicate it has been adopted. Attach a sign with twine or masking tape so as not to harm the tree, or place a sign in the ground.

Make a list of questions for students to answer about the tree so they can get to know it. Students answer the questions by observing the tree and doing research. Ask them to describe the tree; its buds; evidence of disease; clues that animals may be using the tree; any plants growing on the tree; changes that take place in the tree throughout the year; the purpose of its leaves, roots, bark, trunk, buds, flowers, etc., how the tree gets food and water, etc. Ask students to measure the diameter of the trunk and estimate the tree's age and height. After students are familiar with the tree, try some of the following activities:

● Make a crayon bark rubbing.
● Photograph your tree through the seasons and make a display.
● Have a party for the tree.
● Make a model of the tree.
● Make a certificate officially recognizing the adoption of the tree.
● Write poems about the tree.
● Ask a forester or tree expert to visit the class and discuss trees and their proper care. Have the class prune and fertilize the tree, and attend to any of its other needs.
● Write a story about a typical day in the life of your tree.
● Conduct a class period under the tree.

MARK JENNES

Knock! Knock!

Who's there? Orange! Orange who? Orange you glad it's National Humor Month?

Laughter has long been called "the best medicine" for any ailment. To recognize that laughter is an important means to reduce stress, improve performance and enrich the quality of life, April has been declared National Humor Month.

Children love jokes and riddles as much as adults do, and your class is no different! Joke and riddle contests, limerick-writing assignments and book reviews of comedies are ways to celebrate National Humor Month—and keep you chuckling, giggling, guffawing and belly laughing through April!

Humor Me!

Try these rib-tickling activities in honor of National Humor Month.

Hold a limerick "laugh-in." Begin by reading selections from *A Rocket In My Pocket: The Rhymes and Chants of Young Americans,* compiled by Carl Withers (Henry Holt, 1988). Then invite students to put their own feelings and observations into rhyme and share the composition with the class.

Hold a joke-telling hour. Establish a specific time for reading jokes, rhymes, and riddles. Then have students create their own jokes or let them choose a favorite one from a joke book.

Cherish every chuckle! Keep a running list of all the humorous incidents that happen throughout the year. Have kids work in groups to illustrate the incidents and compile the drawings in a class booklet.   PAULA F. MACDONALD

Hey! That's Funny

April is National Humor Month, so get ready for some rib-tickling fun with these writing activities.

Just for Laughs

Imagine you are visiting a planet where people don't know what laughter is. Write a deliver a speech called "How to Laugh." First define what laughter is. Then compare and contrast different kinds of laughs (chuckle, guffaw, snicker, titter, giggle) and demonstrate each.

Joking Around

Collect the favorite jokes of people you know. Organize them by type (knock-knock, elephant, pun, etc.) in a booklet called "My Personal Joke Book." Choose your favorite kind of joke and write some original ones.

Team Time

Work in a team to write a funny skit. Dream up a silly situation or use one of these: 1. Frankenstein's monster is your substitute teacher. 2. Your classroom is beamed aboard an alien spacecraft. 3. You come to school and everybody is speaking in rhyme but you.

Buckets And Bunnies

Create this colorful, Easter Bunny bulletin board to teach abbreviations. Count out eight pastel-colored bunnies from tagboard and add cotton tails, fuzzy pink noses, and eyes. Give each bunny a basket with a different category printed on it, such as "Time," "Weight," "Days of the Week," and so on. Write the abbreviations for each category on miniature cutout eggs, and place them in a folder tacked to the bottom corner of the bulletin board. Students take turns selecting eggs from the envelope and placing them in the corresponding baskets. RHODA T. LONDON

Literary Eggs

As spring rolls around, try this bulletin-board motivator to encourage story reading, mastering new skills, and other independent activities.

First, decorate the background with grass, trees, and flowers. Then count out a human-sized Easter rabbit out of tagboard, decorate it, and paste it on the board. Next, make a three-dimensional paper basket and arrange it over the rabbit's arm.

Every time children finish a picture book or master particular skills, have them cut out, decorate, and write their names on paper eggs. Then put the eggs in the basket. Soon the whole basket will be full, and classroom enthusiasm will really bloom in April! CORDELIA HULL

Sentence Scramblers

Here's an Easter-inspired reading activity to introduce to your class this holiday season. All you'll need are about a dozen plastic Easter eggs and strips of colored tagboard. Then cut up the sentence so that each word is on a separate piece, and place the pieces into one of the plastic eggs. Fill each egg with a sentence and then place them all in the basket.

Each child in a reading group takes an egg and cracks it open to get to the sentence pieces. The children then arrange the pieces to make logical sentences.

JUDY MEAGHER

Hatching Homonyms

This interactive bulletin board is a fun springtime activity. Cut halves of eggs from pastel-colored construction paper. Write halves of homonym pairs on the eggs. Cut baby chicks and their beaks from construction paper. Write the other halves of homonym pairs on the chicks. Staple eggs to the board so chicks can slide easily into them. Put chicks in an envelope attached to the board. Students slide chicks into matching homonym eggs. On the left side of the board, chicks made from yarn balls with construction paper eyes and beaks hatch from eggs made of spring wrapping paper. Use rickrack to enhance the heading.

ATLANTA AREA CENTER FOR TEACHERS

Bluebird Blends

Cut out bluebirds from construction paper and decorate. Make the sun, a tree, an umbrella, cloud and rainbow from construction paper, and write a consonant blend on each. Write word endings such as ipe, ake, etc., on the birds. On the bottom edge of the bulletin board, make construction paper grass which also serves as a pocket to hold the birds. Students pin the bird word endings to a consonant blend sun, rainbow, tree or umbrella to try to make words.

DEBORAH MONTANA

"Some Bunny" Loves This Work

Try this festive holiday display for showcasing students' work. Begin by fashioning a cuddly Easter Bunny from fuzzy white material, then give it a cotton tail, moveable eyes, and a pipe-cleaner nose. Tie a pink ribbon around its neck. Display students' work adjacent to the bunny.

KRISTA STUMP

Deliver The Eggs

Give each child a white, egg-shaped piece of paper to decorate. Have each student write a noun, verb or adjective on each egg. Cut three baskets from paper, or hook a real basket to the board. Label them with a parts of speech category. Use construction paper rabbits for border. Scatter the eggs on the board with push pins. Students read the word on each egg aloud and place the egg in the correct basket.

SUSAN KELLY

Edible Spring Baskets

Kids will enjoy making and nibbling these tasty treats of spring.

Baskets To make eight, 4-inch baskets, use 1/4 cup of margarine, 40 marshmallows, and 5 cups of a crispy rice cereal. Melt the margarine in an electric frying pan at low heat. Add the marshmallows and stir until melted. Unplug the pan, add the cereal, and mix well. Spoon the mixture onto eight squares of waxed paper. Form each portion into a basket complete with handle. You can also use this mixture to form animals, butterflies, and birds.

Grass For each basket, put 2 tablespoons of coconut in a plastic bag. Add a few drops of green food coloring and shake until tinted. Spread onto waxed paper to dry.

Bunny For each bunny, use 2 1/2 marshmallows, three toothpicks, a bowl of water, and red powdered gelatin. Dip the marshmallows in water, then roll in the dry gelatin powder. Fasten two marshmallows together with a toothpick to make the body and head. Cut the remaining half marshmallow into two ears and attach with broken toothpicks. Use a toothpick dipped in food coloring to draw in features. Encourage kids to experiment to make flowers and other animals.

Students assemble their projects, make copies of the recipes, and take home wrapped in clear plastic wrap.

JEAN STANGL

Library Scavenger Hunt

Are your students "library friendly"? In preparation for National Library Month, try this scavenger hunt with your class. Begin by acquainting them with various library reference sources, such as an encyclopedia, almanac, world atlas, and card catalog. Then divide the class into groups of three or four. Give the groups a specific time limit in which to find the following information:

- the winning team of the 1927 World Series
- the distance, in miles, between Earth and Mars
- the author and publication date of the novel, *Pardon Me, You're Stepping on My Eyeball*
- the location of East Germany (longitude and latitude)
- the title of a Cary Grant movie

At the end of this activity, bring the groups together to discuss their answers.

PAULA HAMILTON

Books Abound In April!

April showers bring May flowers, and in the meantime, what better way to wile away those rainy April days than with a good book? National Library Week and International Children's Book Day are the perfect occasions to emphasize the importance of reading.

International Children's Book day commemorates the international aspects of children's literature as well as the birthday of Hans Christian Andersen. To celebrate this special day, have children read some of Andersen's works, illustrate one of his stories or put on a short play based on one of his stories.

National Library Week is a good time to reacquaint children with the library. Take your class on an outing to the local library. Be sure to schedule the visit in advance with the librarian so he or she can spend some time with the students.

For younger students, maybe a story read aloud or a quiet reading time would be a welcomed activity. For older students, an introduction to card and computer catalog skills and the many research and reference materials available is useful. In addition, you may wish to point out the many other services a library offers, such as film showings, lectures and lending items such as cameras, films, recordings, games and even computer programs and equipment.

Spring Into Reading

Grow a garden of good books. Ask kids to create giant, colorful paper flowers and to write on each stem their favorite book for spring reading. As kids think of more titles, your garden will grow.

C.R. FIVVER

Book Hospital

Here's a timesaver to try when students help pack up textbooks and classroom-library books for the summer. To avoid having to examine each book yourself, label two cartons Book Clinic, for books needing minor repairs—new cards, labels—and Book Hospital, for major repairs—broken spines, torn pages. When kids find damaged books, they place them in the appropriate carton. JUDITH WEISS

The House That Books Built

Use National Library Week as a time to acquaint pupils with your community's public library. The following activities will broaden their awareness of this institution as an important community resource.

Ask students to find out how their public library's collection reflects community interests. Is there a special section for books by local authors? Primary-source materials on local heritage? Special programs and services? Are there libraries in your area that house collections of films? Works of art? Photography? Do any local organizations or companies have libraries? Museums? Zoos? Newspaper offices? Are there any specialized libraries—medical, patent, performing arts?

Invite your school librarian and representatives of other local collections to a seminar. Ask guests to give short presentations about their facilities. After a question-and-answer session, follow up with library field trips.

Public libraries are institutions that exemplify democratic living. What do students think libraries have to do with democracy? Are libraries a luxury or a central part of a self-governing society?

What is censorship and what does it have to do with libraries? The Library Bill of Rights states that libraries should provide materials that present all points of view concerning issues of the time. Libraries should challenge censorship as part of their responsibility to provide information.

Ask students how they would react if they found out that a whole section of U.S. history had been omitted from their textbooks and library resources. What if the period of slavery during the Civil War period had been excluded because of one group's denial or another group's shame? Ask students to think of other historical events a specific group might want to censor. Discuss who these people might be and their reasons.

Math

How large is the largest library in the world? The United States Library of Congress takes up 64.6 acres of floor space. Its collections include more than 20 million prints and photographs, 300,000 reels of movies, 3 million volumes of music, and 400,000 newspapers. Make a bar graph that compares the size of the Library of Congress to your school library.

Language Arts

Ask kids to close their eyes while your read this scenario: It's almost dismissal time on Friday, and you've just remembered there's a book report due Monday! You dash down to the library and scan the shelves. Great! A book catches your eye, you flip through the pages, and you're caught. The next time you look up, the library is dark and the door is locked—everyone is gone!

Together, create an exciting escape by enlisting the help of book characters. Who would kids bring to life? What parts of stories might they take advantage of? Will the White Rabbit run by and lead to a special hole to slide through? Are Dorothy and her magic shoes close behind? How about a handy time machine to lend intriguing possibilities? Once outside, how would kids get home? A ride with Mr. Toad? A lift with Mary Poppins?

Ask students to write down their "great escapes," share their stories, and work together to embellish creations. Practice telling your stories, then celebrate Library Week by sharing them with younger classes.

Science

Here are some questions-and-answers to help kids recognize that books are vulnerable to their environments: How long do books remain intact? Most paper made since 1850 contains acid and disintegrates in 25 to 100 years. What are some enemies of books? Fire, dust, moisture, bookworms, neglect, rot. What are some of the newest methods of storing books? Video-discs and compact discs. Almost 25 percent of the Library of Congress are disintegrating. Storage on videodiscs helps preserve items that are too fragile to be handled, such as old documents and rare books. Compact discs are economical, can be linked to home computers, and can store an average of 733 books of 300 pages each. What other innovations can students find out about or predict for libraries of the future?

Divide students into small groups and ask each group to choose a topic that may be considered controversial—such as nuclear energy, nuclear weapons, or what to do about America's homeless. Groups scan resources for information from as many viewpoints as possible and share their findings with the class. Did libraries offer resources with a wide variety of opinions? DON KAPLAN

Name

Work For Wildlife!

Did you know that many animals and plants in the United States are threatened or endangered? Endangered animals include the grizzly bear, otter, panther, prairie dog, bald eagle, and brown pelican. Endangered trees include the Ozark chestnut, St. Helena redwood, and black cabbage tree.

Observe National Wildlife Week by creating a campaign poster to save a threatened or endangered species. The following questions will get you started.

1. Which threatened or endangered animal or plant will you campaign for? (Select one from the list above or one of your own.)

_____

2. What do you already know about the species you have chosen?

FACTS:

1. _____
2. _____
3. _____

3. Find out three more facts about the species from a book or encyclopedia.

FACTS:

1. _____
2. _____
3. _____

4. What kind of poster might alert others to the plight of your plant or animal? What catchy slogan could you use?

_____

_____

_____

5. Make a sketch of your poster on the back of this sheet of paper. If you'd like, use poster paper, markers, and other art supplies to create the real thing.

Writing Assignments To Keep Kids "On The Ball"

Baseball is one of America's favorite games and a sign of spring! If your students can't keep their minds on their work this spring, here are a few writing activities to exercise their language skills and take advantage of baseball fever at the same time!

● Have students use conventional phrases like "to have something on the ball," "to be out in left field," "to be caught off base," "double play," "to strike out," "to get to first base," and "out of my league" in baseball cartoons that they design and write themselves.

● Students choose a role—umpire, manager, outfielder or catcher—and write about the game from that point of view.

● Students make a collection of baseball terms and look them up to find out what they mean. The teacher then includes the words in a puzzle game or word search.

● Students write about the "inner" game of baseball as a baseball owner, scout, player, front office person, sports-writer or a manager of a team.

● In the first World Series between the Boston Red Sox and the Pittsburgh Pirates in 1903, the Red Sox won, 5-3. Pretending to be sports reporters at the World Series, students write a story about the game, using baseball jargon. Have them learn more about the players of both teams, such as Deacon Phillippe (pitcher for the Pirates) and Cy Young (pitcher for the Red Sox). Then ask students to design and write a souvenir program or poster advertising the game.

DOROTHY ZJAWIN

Read And Run

Here's a bulletin board to make in honor of the start of baseball season. Cover a bulletin board with green construction paper and add a baseball diamond outline and two large dugouts. Divide the class into two teams and give each member a construction-paper baseball to "autograph." Each child then places the baseball in his or her team's dugout. Each time a child reads a book, he or she may advance one base. The team that scores the most "runs" at the end of the year wins.   REGINA CABRAL

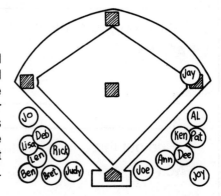

Research Baseball Facts

Not only is April the beginning of baseball season, it is also the month of some interesting baseball facts. On April 11, 1947, Jackie Robinson was the first Black Person to join a major league baseball team. On April 8, 1974, Hank Aaron hit his 715th home run to break Babe Ruth's record of 714 home runs, made 40 years earlier. Aa baseball catcher's mask was worn for the first time on April 12, 1877; and the first U.S. president to pitch a ball to open the baseball season was President Taft on April 14, 1910. Use this baseball interest to promote more research. Have pupils use reference books and sports books to create a class list of baseball firsts. Or, suggest they research some of the baseball greats and create a bulletin board of facts about these persons.

May

- ○ American Bike Month
- ○ Better Sleep Month
- ○ Correct Posture Month
- ○ Mental Health Month
- ○ National Photo Month
- ○ National Physical Fitness Month
- ○ National Sightsaving Month

Movable Events

First full week—Be Kind to Animals Week
First full week—National Pet Week
First full week—Asian-Pacific American Heritage Week
First Sunday and first full week—National Family Week

Second Sunday—Mother's Day
Sunday of Memorial Day Weekend—Indianapolis 500
Last Monday—Memorial Day

Red Letters Day

1. This is an important day in many countries. Find out about May Day celebrations in the Soviet Union, Great Britain, Finland and other countries.

2. Elijah McCoy, born in 1844 in Canada, invented the lubricator cup. His invention dripped oil continuously to oil machinery parts so they did not have to be shut down. Soon companies insisted that real McCoy cups be used on all machines purchased. The expression "the real McCoy" is still with us. What does it mean?

3. The World's Columbian Exposition opened in Chicago in 1893. Often called "the White City," the exposition used more electricity than the whole of Chicago at that time. Make a list of ways to save electricity.

4. Today is National Weather Observer's Day. What will the weather be tomorrow?

5. Cinco de Mayo. This Mexican national holiday remembers the Battle of Puebla on May 5, 1862. Research this important day.

6. This is the halfway point of spring—there are as many days until summer begins as have passed since the last day of winter. Are you looking forward to summer? Tell why.

7. We can thank Edwin H. Land, born in 1909, for inventing a camera that takes and develops a picture in seconds. Read to find out about some of his other inventions.

8. Jean H. Dunant, a Swiss, was born in 1828. He founded the International Red Cross. Read more about him.

9. James M. Barrie, born in 1860, was a English author. His play *Peter Pan* is set in Never-Never Land, a place where no one grows up. What would it be like never to grow up?

10. Radios are so common today we don't even think about a time when they didn't exist. But there was excitement on this day in 1927, when the Hotel Statler in Boston, Massachusetts offered two radio channels to guests. Thirteen hundred rooms were equipped with headsets for one person to listen at a time. Enjoy a radio program today.

11. Today, in 1947, the B. F. Goodrich Company started to manufacture tubeless tires. Look up *tire* in an encyclopedia to find out what tires were like before tubeless ones were invented.

12. Limerick Day. Find out the rhyme scheme for a limerick and then try your hand at writing one.

13. Stevie Wonder, was born in 1951. Listen to some of his recordings today.

14. Midnight Sun at North Cape. Find North Cape, Norway on a map and see how far north it is. From May 14 until July 30, the sun never goes below the horizon at this island.

15. Ellen Church, a trained nurse, became the first airplane stewardess on this day in 1930. What are stewardesses called today? Are they always women?

15. A "Keedoozle" store, opened in Memphis, Tennessee in 1937. Items to be sold were in rows covered with glass. Customers would insert a notched rod into a keyhole beside each item they wanted. When the customer had made all the purchases, he or she inserted the rod in a final slot and all the items were released onto a conveyor belt for wrapping. What would be the advantage of such a store? The disadvantage?

16. In 1866, Congress authorized the creation of the nickel, the five-cent piece. Look at a nickel and describe it.

17. Happy Birthday, New York Stock Exchange. In 1792, about two dozen merchants and brokers agreed to form a group for buying and selling stocks. Read to find out what the stock exchange does.

18. On this day in 1980, the Mount St. Helens volcano in Washington State erupted. Find out what a volcano is and why it erupts.

19. Dark Day in New England. At midday in 1780, the sky in New England suddenly became dark. No one is sure why this happened. Why do you think it may have happened?

20. Dolley Madison was born today in 1768. She was the wife of James Madison, fourth president of the United States. Find out more about this important woman.

20. Do you like tossed salad? Then you would have liked to have been at the Salinas Fair in California in 1988. Seventeen ingredients including 47,250 heads of iceberg lettuce, were used to make a huge salad. Ask your mother if you can celebrate the event with salad for supper.

21. An early aviation pioneer, Glenn H. Curtiss, was born in 1878. He helped design a plane, called the *June Bug,* which in 1909 was the first plane sold commercially. It cost $5,000. Find out more about the work of this amazing man.

22. National Maritime Day. In 1819, the ship *Savannah,* left Savannah, Georgia for Liverpool, England, the first steamship to cross the Atlantic. Find out more about it.

23. On this day in 1903, a doctor and a mechanic left San Francisco by car. They arrived in New York City on July 26. Read about early automobiles and roads to learn some of the problems they probably encountered on the trip.

24. In 1983, hundreds of people walked across the Brooklyn Bridge in New York City. They were celebrating the 100th anniversary of the opening of this bridge to traffic. Read about it in an encyclopedia to find why it was called "the eighth wonder of the world."

25. National Missing Children's Day. Use today to learn what to do if someone you do not know wants to talk to you, give you a lift, or give you a present.

26. John Wayne, was born today in 1907. When he was asked what advice he had for young actors, he said, "Talk low, talk slow, and don't say too much." Was this good advice?

27. We can thank Rachel Carson, born in 1907, for many of the laws we have today against using poisonous chemicals. Ask at the library for a book about her life.

28. Jim Thorpe, born in 1886, was one of the world's most versatile athletes. He played professional football, won fame as a track-and-field champion, and played major-league baseball. Find out more about him.

29. In 1916, President Wilson created an order for the design of the President's Flag. Look up *flag* in an encyclopedia to find pictures of these flags. Select one and describe it to a friend.

30. Traditional Memorial Day. What Memorial Day activities are there in your town?

31. In 1933, a patent was given to Gerald Brown for making "invisible" glass. Why do you think there was a need for glass to be "invisible"? Actually, the patent was for a process that would reduce the amount of reflection on glass windows. Why would someone, especially a storekeeper, want to get rid of reflections on glass?

May Writing Activities

The following writing activities will add some spice to your writing program as the year winds down. You can assign one activity each week or let pupils choose those they wish to pursue.

● Is there "a place where dreams are born"? Certainly. Sir James M. Barrie created it in the novel *Peter Pan.* His Never-Never Land included a mystical Mermaid's Lagoon, a dangerous but beautiful forest, and some highly suspicious pirate ships. Celebrate his May 9th birthday by designing your own personal magical kingdom. What enchantments are alluring to you?

● The first Academy Awards were presented on May 16, 1929. If you had been a founding member of the Academy of Motion Picture Arts and Sciences, which awards the "Oscar" statuettes, what criteria would you have suggested for selecting Best Picture? What are your five all-time favorite movies?

● Memorial Day, observed the last Monday in May, honors those who died fighting for our country. Can you imagine what it would be like to fight in a war? Record your thoughts. If possible, talk to people who have had the experience.

● May is a perfect month to make a pledge to get fit—it's National Physical Fitness and Sports Month! Choose an exercise—situps, jumping jacks, pull-ups—make sure you know how to do the exercise correctly, then section off several sheets of paper for record-keeping. Or ask your P.E. teacher to help you set up an exercise program.

● You've heard of new year's resolutions? Why not make a few summertime resolutions? List at least five things you hope you'll do this summer—like make a new friend, start a new hobby, or get more exercise. Use a journal to remind you of your summer plans.

Mother Goose Day

May 1 is Mother Goose Day. Who was Mother Goose? Legend has it that Mother Goose was actually several people—not just one—who wrote rhyming verses and compiled them in a single volume of poems. To celebrate this special day, start by reading aloud several rhymes or have kids take turns reading to classmates. Use the rhymes as a starting point for a discussion on the different rhyming patterns found in the verses.

● Give students different Mother Goose verses to which they must add their own lines, following the established rhyme pattern. Or assign particular patterns, such as those found in "Mary Had a Little Lamb," or "Hey Diddle Diddle," and have children write verses of their own using that rhyme pattern.

As a drama activity, divide the class into groups and assign a different nursery rhyme to each. Give groups about five minutes in which to decide how they will act out their given nursery rhyme. The sillier the better!

● For an art activity, have students draw their own impressions of specific Mother Goose characters. Afterwards, pass around an illustrated edition of the Mother Goose rhymes for comparison.   GLORIA T. DELAMAR

The Many Faces Of May 1

The many aspects of May 1 are good research projects. Observed as a holiday since ancient times, early celebrations included spring festivals and Maypole dances. Then it became a day to honor workers. Even today, it is a workers' holiday in socialist countries. In the United States, May 1 is observed as Law Day or Loyalty Day. Have pupils research May Day celebrations through the years to create an illustrated time line of the many ways it has been observed.

Name _____

Lay Down The Law!

May 1 is Law Day—a time we stop to recognize the importance of a fair and just legal system. Be your own legal eagle. Pick up your lawmaker's pen and lay down your own laws.

1. If you have children of your own one day, what family rules will you have about bedtime, chores, allowance, behavior, and so on? _____

_____

_____

_____

2. What problem in your neighborhood, school, town, or state would you like to help solve? _____

_____

Would a law help? _____

If so, what would you like the law to say? _____

_____

_____

_____

3. If you could write a law that every person in every country in the world had to obey, what would it be? _____

_____

_____

_____

Why do you think this law is important? _____

_____

Not Just Fun And Games

Come May, my students start thinking of fun and games, so I channel their interests into this whole-class activity. We make a class booklet about traditional indoor and outdoor games, containing facts, historical information, playing instructions, trivia, and so on. This activity reinforces language and research skills, physical coordination, and the value of cooperation. It also gives kids something tangible to take home with them at the end of the year.

We start by listing a number of traditional games, such as hopscotch, tag, jump rope, marbles, jacks, dominoes, Chinese checkers, and so on. Then we review the rules and playing instructions for each game. Wherever possible, I bring in samples of the games for kids to see and use. Then I assign children specific games to research and have them write short essays summarizing their findings.

Finally, I assemble all the essays in a booklet and make enough copies for all the students. One day before the end of the school year I set up a game center, allowing the children to move freely from one game to another. I display the rules and history of each game for reference.

On the last day of school, kids take the booklets home and continue their fun and games throughout the summer break!
DORIS DILLON

Be Kind To Animals Week

Celebrate Be Kind to Animals Week with the American Humane Association's *Be Kind to Animals Activities* manual. The manual, which includes story starters, worksheets, art project ideas, and more, is available for $5 from the American Humane Association, P.O. Box 1266, Denver, CO 80201-1266.

Be Kind To Animals Week

Teach your class about the responsibility and joy of owning a pet for Be Kind to Animals Week. Discuss proper feeding, grooming, love, exercise and health care for animals, as well as how to determine what kind of pet to get (busy children may want to keep fish or hamsters, because they require feeding and cage or aquarium upkeep, but do not need a lot of attention like puppies).

It's A Dog's Life

In recognition of Be Kind to Animals Week, and to give students a better understanding of dogs, their contributions to society, and the duties and responsibilities of dog owners, declare a special Dog Day in your classroom. Invite members of your community with dog-related professions to talk to your class. Possibilities include a representative from a dog-grooming service, the owner of a show dog, a trainer of police or seeing-eye dogs, representatives from a local dog-obedience school or animal shelter, or a dog breeder.

Follow up guests' visits by having students bring in pictures of their own dogs or dogs from magazines, and then create a bulletin board to showcase these special pictures. As a combined research and art project, ask students to choose a specific breed to research, and have them make a poster illustrating the dog in action. As a creative-writing activity, have students write fantastical essays about dogs. Suggest wacky titles, such as "The Poodle Who Ran For President," "Marvin the Mutt Goes to the Moon," and so on. Encourage children to share their essays with the class.
JEAN STANGL

Animals, Animals, Animals!

Be Kind to Animals Week in May is a reminder to us all to treat our animal friends with love and respect. Think about your responsibility to animals as you try these writing activities.

A Bird's-Eye View

Pretend you are a dog, a cat, a parakeet or another family pet. Write a journal entry from the animal's point of view. Tell about your typical day and what you think of your owners and other animals in your neighborhood.

Animal Crack-Ups

What's your favorite comic strip animal? Do you think Snoopy is super or Garfield is great? Write and draw an original comic strip using your favorite cartoon animal. Or you can create a furry or feathered hero of your own.

Team Time

Work in a team to design and create a poster to remind people to be kind to animals. Use a catchy slogan to help get your message across.

All Creatures Great And Small

Animals have brought people pleasure as pets and companions for thousands of years. Say thank you to our animal friends during Be Kind to Animals Week with these activities.

Choose Me!

People often read newspaper ads when looking for pets. Imagine that pets could read newspaper ads looking for owners! Write a classified ad about yourself. Tell what kind of pet owner you would be and what kind of pet you would like to have choose you.

Wild and Tame

Read this quotation by French writer Antoine de Saint-Exupéry: "You become responsible forever, for what you have tamed." Write a paragraph telling what the quotation means to you and why it applies to having a pet.

Team Time

Work with a friend to write a letter to a local animal shelter or organization, requesting information on pet adoption. Find out the specifics involved in adopting a pet. Then share what you've learned with your classmates.

American Bike Month

Get your class geared up for American Bike Month, which focuses on bicycle safety. The National Safety Council offers a comprehensive bicycle driver's test, which includes questions on bicycle safety and maintenance, traffic regulations, and more. For a copy of the bicycle driver's test, or for more information on American Bike Month, contact the National Safety Council, Community Safety Programs Group, 444 N. Michigan Ave., Chicago, IL 60611.

Shoot For Great Work

In recognition of National Physical Fitness and Sports Month, try this sportsminded bulletin board. Cover a bulletin board with a green background and trim with an orange border. Then attach a basketball hoop (like the kind found in most toy stores) and place a foam basketball inside. Every time students complete assignments correctly, give them construction-paper basketballs with their names printed on them. Students then attach the cutouts to the bulletin board as if they are "shooting" for the hoop.   LU ALICE KAMPWERTH

Bikes Are Beautiful

Are you a bike fan? If so, you've got lots of company—more Americans are riding bikes than ever before. Become a better bicyclist by brushing up on bike traffic and safety rules during American Bike Month.

Riding by the Book

Find out about the bicycle laws, rules, and regulations in your community. Then design a poster illustrating one law, rule, or regulation. Create a slogan that will catch people's attention. Ask your principal if you may display your poster in school.

Spectacular Spokes

Write a story for younger children about a bicycle with magical powers. Include a complete description of the bike. Add illustrations if you'd like. Try to include information that will teach younger children about bike safety.

Team Time

Work in a group to write a consumer guide about bicycles. In your guide, describe the types of bikes available and how much each one costs. Inform your readers about any safety problems associated with each brand. Illustrate the guide and share it with your classmates.

Name _____

Hey, Sport!

   May is National Physical Fitness and Sports Month. Give your brain a workout by finding and circling each sport in the word search.

Riddle: Why was the piano tuner hired to play on the baseball team?

Answer: Because he had ___ ___ ___ ___ ___ ___ ___ ___   ___ ___ ___ ___ ___ ___

Find the answer by filling in the blanks with numbered letters in the word search.

B	A	S	E²	B	A	L	L	S	B		**basketball**
I	R	O	H	O	C¹¹	K	E	Y	A		**polo**
K	C⁶	C	J	W	R	S	T	R³	S		**bowling**
I	H¹²	C	U	L	I	K	E	U	K		**judo**
N	E	E	D	I	V	I⁹	N	G	E⁵		**biking**
G	R	R	O	N	A	I	N	B	T¹⁰		**diving**
X	Y	G	P¹	G	C	N	I	Y	B		**sailing**
O	B	G	O	L	F	G	S	N	A		**skiing**
S	A	I	L	I	N	G	P⁸	G	L		**baseball**
I	N	F⁴	O	O	T⁷	B	A	L	L		**tennis**

basketball
polo
bowling
judo
biking
diving
sailing
skiing
baseball
tennis
football
rugby
golf
soccer
archery
hockey

Gold Star Ideas
★ See how many new words you can find by using the letters in the word basketball. Here are three words to start you off: ask, bet, and table.
★★ Look for this book in the library: *Bodyworks: The Kids Guide to Food and Physical Fitness* by Carol Bershad and Deborah Bernick (Random House, 1981).

Greetings, Mom

A great idea for a Mother's Day gift that kids can make easily and independently is a set of note cards. Start with five ready-made envelopes. Cut paper to fit easily into envelopes when folded in half. Have kids use watercolor paint or a stamp pad to put a thumb print or two on the front of the paper. When the paper is dry, have kids use their imaginations to add a few black lines with a fine-tipped black marker. You'll see that a simple thumbprint can be transformed into an adorable mouse, a lovely maiden, or a fat caterpillar! Children can either make all the cards uniform or each one unique. The result is a delightful set of notecards for mom.

MARGARET GROTE

Folding Poems

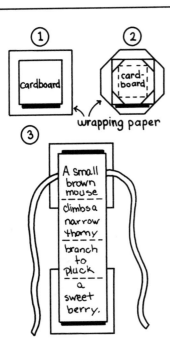

Fold-books make great holiday gifts for kids to give. First, students write drafts of original poems or seasonal greetings. Then, each student copies the corrected, finished version onto a 2 1/2-by-10-inch piece of paper. Fold each paper into quarters—2 1/2 inches by 2 1/2 inches.

To prepare a cover for the fold-book, the child glues one side of a 3-inch-square piece of cardboard to the center of a 5-inch-square piece of wrapping paper. (See figure 1.) Next, the student folds the wrapping paper over the corners and edges of the cardboard (as shown in figure 2) and glues it in place. The child then tapes a 12-inch length of ribbon in the center of one cardboard so that both ends dangle freely.

To complete the book, the student glues the top quarter of the poem onto one piece of covered cardboard and the bottom quarter against a second piece of cardboard. (See figure 3.) Let the books dry overnight. Then refold each book and tie with ribbon.

PAMELA HEUKEROIL

Mother's Day Flower

Combine language skills and art with this touching gift for Mother's Day. Cut out large flower parts from colored construction paper. There should be six large petals, a center circle, a large stem and two leaves. Glue a snapshot of the child's mother onto the center circle. On each petal, have each child write an adjective that describes the child's mother. Use words such as caring, pretty, helpful, sweet, best, etc. Print the phrase "I love you" down the stem. Every mother will enjoy receiving this personalized card!

JUDY KEEPORTS

Name _____

Mother's Day At The Zoo!

Write the correct baby animal name next to the grown-up animal name. Use the baby animal names in the box to help you. You may also use a dictionary. The first one has been done for you.

Grown-up animal name	**Baby animal name**	**Baby animal names**
1. kangaroo	j o e y	calf
2. cat		chick
3. elephant		cygnet
4. horse		elver
5. sheep		eyas
6. dog		foal
7. turkey		~~joey~~
8. swan		kid
9. eel		kitten
10. hawk		lamb
11. chicken		poult
12. goat		puppy
13. hog		shoat

Baby animal name (with numbered blanks):
j(2) o e(15) y
___ ___ ___ ___ ___ (10)
___ ___ ___ (14)
___ ___ (7)
___ ___ (6)
___ ___ (3)
___(4) ___ ___ ___(8)
___ ___(5)
___ ___ ___ ___(11)
___ ___ ___(12)
___(1) ___ ___
___ ___ ___(13)
___ ___ ___ ___(9)

Riddle: What did the joey write in the card he gave to his mom?
To find the answer, write the numbered letters above on the lines below!

___ ___ ___ ___ ___   ___ ___ ___ ___ ___ ___ ___ ,   ___ ___ ___ ___ !
1   2   3   4   5   6   7   8   9 10 11 12   13 14 15

Gold Star Ideas

★ Many animals have male and female names. For example, a male sheep is a ram and a female sheep is a ewe. Use an encyclopedia to find the male and female names for as many animals as you can.

★★ Write a story called "Mother's Day at the Zoo." Begin the story when a mixed-up zookeeper puts the wrong baby animals and mothers together!

To The Top Of The World

What does the world look like from the top of the world's highest mountain? That's what Edmund Hillary and Tenzing Norgay found out on May 29, 1953, when they reached the top of Mount Everest. Join in the spirit of adventure with these writing activities.

Choose an Adventure

If you could go anywhere in the world on an adventure, where would it be? Choose a spot that intrigues you. Write down five facts you know about the place. Then do some research in the library. Write down five facts you learn from your research.

Welcome To...

Many writers have created imaginary places where life is perfect. These are called utopias. Write a story in which an explorer discovers your idea of utopia.

Team Time

What geographical points of interest or historical sights are located in your city or state? Work in a team to create a travel brochure.

Peace In Our World

Include in your observance of Memorial Day, some thoughts of peace, with the hope that, in the future, men and women will not need to fight for freedom and perhaps lose their lives. These activities will help to focus pupils' ideas on the importance of peace in our world.

● Teach children to write "peace" in several languages. Students then write the words on construction paper, cut the words out, attach a string or piece of yarn, and hang them from a coat hanger for a mobile.

● Ask students to write poems or stories about peace. Display them in a prominent place in the classroom or library.

● Encourage students to write to their legislators and heads of state about peace issues.

● Keep a class scrapbook of news stories about people working for peace, including Nobel Peace Prize winners, foreign dignitaries and religious leaders. ELLEN HASBROUCK

Flag-Waving Fun

Celebrate Memorial Day with these easy-to-make flags. Fold an 8 1/2-by-11-inch white paper in half lengthwise, then in half again widthwise. Unfold paper, then cut off and discard one quarter. To form the "flagpole," fold the 8 1/2-inch side in half lengthwise, then in half lengthwise again, leaving the flag quarter free. Tape to secure. Decorate with stars and stripes. Now wave your flags to Sousa's "Stars and Stripes Forever." PENNY CARTER

Memorial Day

Take time out today to reflect on the American men and women who lost their lives in battle, fighting for freedom. Encourage students to send cards or letters to a veterans' hospital in your area.

June

- ○ American Rivers Month
- ○ June Dairy Month
- ○ National Adopt-a-Cat Month
- ○ National Tennis Month
- ○ Zoo and Aquarium Month

Movable Events

First Sunday—Family Day
First full Week—National Safe Boating Week
Second Saturday—Queen's (Elizabeth II) Official Birthday
Second Sunday—Children's Sunday

Week including June 14—National Flag Week
Week beginning second Monday—National Little League Baseball Week
Third Sunday—Father's Day
About June 21—Summer Begins

Red Letter Days

1. On this day in 1813, Captain James Lawrence's ship *Chesapeake* was in a battle against the British ship *Shannon* during the War of 1812. Captain Lawrence was wounded badly during the battle but he kept urging his men along. "Don't give up the ship," was his dying comment. This statement became the watchword of the U.S. Navy, and many people today use it. When might you have said the statement?

2. A swimming pool built in the White House, was formally accepted and opened by President Franklin Roosevelt in 1933. Read about this president's life and why a swimming pool was more than just entertainment for him.

3. The ballad "Casey at the Bat," was first printed in the *San Francisco Examiner* on June 3, 1888. This poem is still read and enjoyed, over one hundred years later. Find a copy and read it aloud to the class.

4. In 1781, Jack Jouett rode 45 miles for 6 1/2 hours to warn Virginia's Governor Thomas Jefferson and the legislature that the British were coming. You might like to write a poem about Mr. Jouett's ride.

5. World Environment Day. On this day activities are held to show concern for the preservation and enhancement of the environment. What can you do today to enhance the environment of your neighborhood?

6. In 1932, the U.S. government passed a law that placed a tax of one cent a gallon on gasoline and other motor fuel. Ask at a gas station how much the federal gasoline tax is.

7. Gwendolyn Brooks, born in 1917, is a well-known black poet. See if you can find her book *Bronzeville Boys and Girls.* Read a poem you like to the class.

8. Barbara Bush, born in 1925, is the wife of President George Bush (born June 12, 1924). Wives of presidents are called First Ladies. Why?

9. A short cartoon appeared on this day in 1934. One of the characters in it is still a favorite—Donald Duck. Read about Walt Disney, the man responsible for the development of animated films.

10. Sing "Happy Birthday" to Maurice Sendak, born in 1928. Sendak is the illustrator and author of many books you may know. Including *Where the Wild Things Are.* Look in the library for other books he wrote or illustrated.

11. The French oceanographer, Jacque

Cousteau, was born today in 1910. Find out more about him.

12. In 1967, a Soviet space capsule landed on the surface of the planet Venus. Look up this planet and find out two interesting facts about it.

13. On this day in 1966, the U.S. Supreme Court ruled that, when someone is arrested, he or she doesn't have to say anything until a lawyer is present. These rights are called "the Miranda Rights." Why are these rights important?

14. Flag Day. Will your school do something special?

15. Idaho Pioneer Day. The first permanent white settlement, at Franklin, Idaho was settled today in 1860. Find out when your town was settled.

16. Today is a good day to yell. In fact, it's so great that a tiny settlement called Spivey's Corner in North Carolina sponsors a hollerin' contest. Find this town on a map of North Carolina.

17. Barry Manilow, born in 1946, is a well-known singer, composer, and arranger. Look him up in *Who's Who in America.*

18. In 1988, fourteen students at Hanover High School, New Hampshire finished their game of leapfrog. It had started on June 10 and lasted for 189 hours and 49 minutes. It had covered 888.1 miles, long enough to make the *Guiness Book of World Records.* Find this book in the library.

19. A famous comic strip character first appeared today in 1978. Sing "Happy Birthday" to Garfield. Describe what he did in today's comic strip.

20. To celebrate the coming summer season, Fairbanks, Alaska has a midnight sun baseball game that begins about 10:30 P.M. and is played without artificial lights. Look in the paper to see how many hours of daylight there are in your city today.

21. Daniel Carter Beard, born in 1850, helped to found Boy Scouting in the United States and was its first National Commissioner from 1910 until his death in 1941. Ask a scout to tell you about the scouting activities he does.

22. Journalist Ed Bradley, was born today in 1941. You can usually see him on the Sunday night "60 Minutes" program. Who is your favorite newsperson?

23. Irving S. Cobb, born in 1876, was a humorous writer of short stories and novels. He believed that "you had to poke fun at yourself before you could poke fun at anyone else without hurting his feelings." What did he mean? Do you agree?

24. Gustavus Franklin Swift was born on this day in 1839. At 17, he went into the butchering business. Swift went to Chicago and opened the first slaughterhouse there in 1875. Which would be cheaper: to ship meat from Chicago to the East or to transport live animals there? Why?

25. Today, in 1876, General George Custer and his army met a large band of Sioux and Cheyenne Indians. During the battle, Custer and his entire group were killed, as well as a large number of the Indians. The Battleground is now a national monument. Find it on a map of Montana.

26. Today, in 1959, the St. Lawrence Seaway was dedicated and officially opened. Find the St. Lawrence River on a map and trace, with your finger, the route an ocean liner would take to reach Duluth.

27. James Smithson, who died today in 1829, left his great wealth to start a museum in Washington D.C. under the name of the "Smithsonian Institution." Have you ever visited it?

28. On this day in 1925, Irene McFarland was testing a new kind of parachute but was also wearing a regular army one. The new parachute became caught in the plane's fuselage so she hung there, swinging back and forth. But when she opened her regular chute it broke the cords of the new one and her life was saved! Think how you would feel if you were caught hanging there?

29. In 1956, a college freshman made sports history. Charles Dumas was the first person to make a high jump of seven feet, one-half inch. Look in a world almanac or other reference book to see who holds the record today. How high is it?

30. On this day in 1908, a huge meteorite landed in central Siberia. People as far away as 466 miles saw it in full daylight; its blast was felt 50 miles away. Look up *meteor* in an encyclopedia to find out about other places where meteors have struck the earth.

Flag Day

On June 14, 1777, in Philadelphia, Pennsylvania, John Adams introduced a resolution before the Continental Congress stating, "... that the flag of the thirteen United States shall be thirteen stripes, alternate red and white; that the 'Union' be thirteen stars, white in a blue field, representing a new constellation."

Summer Begins

Although school may not be officially out yet, welcome the summer season by taking your class on a neighborhood field trip or conduct a schoolwide scavenger hunt—and get a head start on summer fun!

American Rivers Month

Take time out to enjoy one of America's greatest natural resources—our rivers and streams—during American Rivers Month. As a special tribute, American Rivers Inc. is also offering a full-color poster of Colorado's Rio Grande by nature photographer David Muench. The poster is available for $10. To order, or for more information on what's going on in your area, write to American Rivers, Inc., 801 Pennsylvania Ave., S.E., Suite 400, Washington, DC 20003, or call (202) 547-6900.

Super Summer

It's Summer! Anticipate the fun times ahead with these writing ideas.

It's a Date

Make your own personal calendar of summer fun. Include birthdays of friends and family, as well as special plans, such as vacations and family get-togethers. If you're going to take swimming lessons, for example, note the specific day, time, and place of each lesson. If you'd like to form a club, put on a play, or hold a pet show, jot down some ideas about when and where the big events are to take place. Around the border of your calendar, write words that describe summer. Add illustrations. Post your calendar in your room at home.

Summer Is...

Write a poem that expresses your feelings about this spectacular season. Write the word *summer* vertically—with each letter on a different line. Then make sure that the first word of each line of your poem begins with the letter on that line. Post your poem on a summer bulletin board or in your room at home.

Team Time

Work with a group to write a summer-safety booklet. Include tips on hiking, swimming, biking, and exposure to the sun. Duplicate copies and provide one copy for each group member.

Name _____

Long May It Wave!

On June 14, 1777, the Continental Congress agreed that the flag of the United States would have 13 stripes to represent a "new constellation" in the world of nations. The flag's colors are believed to represent the following: red, courage and strength; white, purity; and blue, vigilance, perseverance, and justice. Celebrate Flag Day—June 14—with these high-flying activities.

● Does your school have a flag? If it does, redesign it using new colors and symbols. If it doesn't, create one. What colors would you use? Would you add a slogan? What would it be?

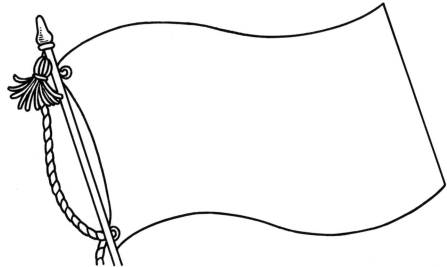

● Create your own personal flag. Use symbols, words, and colors that have special meaning to you. Or, create a family flag using symbols, phrases, colors, and events that represent your family.

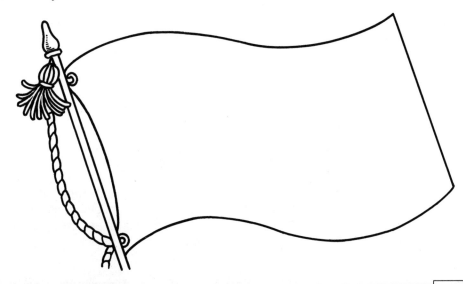

Who's On First

Slide into the season with these winning activities.

● Have your class research the lives of baseball greats, such as Ty Cobb, Babe Ruth, Lou Gehrig, Jackie Robinson, Joe DiMaggio, Hank Aaron, Ted Williams, Mickey Mantle, and so on. Then have children pretend to be the players they've researched when they present their reports to the class. You might even suggest that the kids dress up for the event. Encourage them to include photographs and illustrations of their chosen players to share with the class.

● As a math activity, conduct a lesson on averages using baseball statistics from the *World Almanac* or any other book containing baseball facts, such as *Baseball Rules in Pictures* by G. Jacobs and J.R. McCrory (Perigee Books, 1990). Teach students how to find a player's batting average (the number of base hits, divided by the number of official times at bat), or choose a specific year and have kids compare the batting averages, home runs, or runs batted in of several popular players.

● As a writing activity, have students choose a specific object or person found in a baseball stadium and write about it from the object's or person's point of view. Examples include a day in the life of a hot-dog vendor or what it's like to be third base, the pitcher's mound, or a baseball in flight. Invite children to share their essays with the class.

DANIEL ALPERIN

Happy Father's Day

It's Dad's big day! Praise your pop with the following writing activities.

Think Big

This Father's Day delight your dad with a great big poster! Begin by drawing a large picture of your father's face. Then add a few snappy words of praise underneath it. You might want to experiment with rhyme, puns, alliteration, and other forms of word play. Here are some examples to get you started: "My dad is baaaddd!" and "My pop's the tops!" Create your own thoughtful sayings, then present the poster to Dad, along with a BIG hug on his special day.

Please Advise...

There are lots of books that give advice to parents on how to deal with their kids. But how about a book by and for kids with advice on how to get along with parents? Write five tips on how kids can understand, appreciate, and work cooperatively with their moms and dads. Then organize your work into a class booklet and distribute it to your classmates.

My pop's the tops.

Team Time

Work with a classmate to research the role of fathers in the animal kingdom. Find out what part the males of several different species play in the care, feeding, and rearing of their offspring. You might want to begin by conducting research on penguins, foxes, and chimpanzees. Report your findings to the class.

Classroom Art Gallery

To show off students' masterpieces, both visual and written, create a classroom art gallery. First, divide the back wall of your classroom into as many 18-by-18-inch squares as there are children in the class. Form squares by taping strips of black construction paper to the wall. To identify the squares, have each child sign his or her name on a small piece of tagboard and place it at the bottom of a square. Then, after children have completed a writing or art project, they may display the finished product in their squares.

This gives each child recognition for his or her work of the past year.

JEANNE PETERMEIER

Eat And Go

Need a going-away gift that will express your appreciation and help a student teacher, volunteer, or parent helper remember their days in your classroom? Invite this special person to a farewell party. Early in the day, cover the refreshments table with a sheet of white oilcloth. Before the party, ask each child in the class to write or draw a thank-you message on the cloth, using colorful, waterproof markers or crayons. After the party, your honored guest can then take home this unique memento. NICKI PARSONS

Personal Time Capsules

To help students preserve a bit of the school year, have them make their own time capsules.

About a month before school ends, kids collect empty potato chip canisters. They decorate the canisters with drawings, collages, photographs, and so on. For the next few weeks children select items to store in their time capsules. These items should represent the school year—an A test paper, a friendship bracelet, a flier from a school play, and so on.

On the last day of school, kids seal their canisters, take them home, and store them in secret places. Then, whenever they open them, whether in three months or ten years, the memories come flowing back.

DORIS DILLON

To Whom It May Concern

One of my students' favorite ways to wrap up the school year is by writing welcome letters to next year's class. This activity gives students a reason to reflect on the past year, and reinforces their writing skills too. Here's how we do it:

First we review the year's events, choosing from among such highlights as our favorite field trip, an especially intriguing study unit, a school play, or an unusual class event.

After we've made a comprehensive list, students briefly describe the high points in their letters. Sometimes they include lists of classroom rules and regulations, what they liked or disliked about their teacher, classmates, or subjects, and how they felt about the year in general.

Once students have completed their letters and I've checked them for errors, we seal the letters and place them in a big basket at the front of the room, where they'll remain until fall.

On the first day of school, I distribute the letters to my new students. This personal touch seems to make the transition to a new classroom a bit easier. I also find that former pupils often drop by to see how the new kids on the block are doing. MARY ANN BRENSEL

What A Year!

Kids can review the year by making yearbooks. Fold an 81/2-by-11-inch paper in half. Kids decorate the cover, titling it *My Yearbook.* On a page labeled *Things I Learned To Do This Year,* students write their individual achievements or dictate them to you or an aide. Entitle the next page *My friends are...* and pass the books for all to sign. On the back, kids complete and illustrate the sentence *I liked...*
VIOLET JOHNSON

On The Road To Summer

This end-of-the-year bulletin board gives younger children the opportunity to show off their best work. First cover a bulletin board with yellow butcher paper and trim with a rickrack border. Then make a construction-paper road extending across the board. On the side of the road, attach cutouts of trees, a pond with sailboats, and a bright yellow sun. Next, give pupils cutout cars to decorate and attach to the road. Finally, have students select examples of their best work to post underneath their cars on the bulletin board. Title the board "On the Road to Summer," and bid your class a merry farewell. MARY HUGHES

Good-Bye Gazette

Whether kids are going on to another school or moving up a grade level, it's the time of the year for memories. As a culminating activity, put together a special class yearbooklet. Start things off with a name-the-book contest. Organize a staff to decide events you'll highlight. Ask kids to contribute original poems and stories. Include a Memory Page—kids can interview each other and the staff for personal recollections. On the last page, leave space for addresses and summer good wishes. MARY ELLEN SWITZER

Write An Award

June brings the awards ceremonies that mark the end of another school year. In addition to receiving awards, children may have fun creating an award to give to a famous person in history. When studying science or social studies, discuss significant contributions historical figures have made that have affected our culture. Students then write awards, citing the contributions that changed history.

For example, here's a citation to Columbus: "Congratulations, Columbus! You have earned this award for courage, skill, and leadership. Your heroic efforts from August through October of 1492 have changed the course of history. While trying to reach the West Indies, you discovered a new continent. Thanks to you, many people..."

Encourage children to include four or five items they feel are the most important. They may want to design a certificate to go with their writing to place on display.
TOM BERNAGOZZI

Countdown To Summer

Here's a way to channel children's vacation anticipation. Above a figure of a paper clown, staple real or paper balloons, numbered from one to the number of remaining school days. Connect balloons to the clown's hands with yarn. At the end of each day, remove the highest numbered balloon. Leave the yarn to show another day gone by.

ROSEMARY ADKINS

Heading Out For Summer Fun

This bright bulletin board gets students in gear for summer. Have each student cut out a car from construction paper and write his or her name and summertime destination on it. Post the cars on the bulletin board highways for all to see.

ATLANTA AREA CENTER FOR TEACHERS

Where Are You Going?

When it's almost time for school to end for the summer, I conduct a class discussion on summer plans, both students' and my own. I first ask kids to bring in travel brochures, postcards, photographs, and other materials that tell about the places they plan or hope to visit during the summer break. We then look up the locations on the map and discuss what each destination is best known for. I also encourage students to keep summer vacation journals to record their adventures and experiences. Since I keep one too, I share my adventures with the class in order to give them a bit of prewriting inspiration.

JACKIE SLADE

And Then He Said...

Here's a great way to encourage kids to read this summer. It may sound a bit sneaky, but it works every time!

During the last month of school, I choose two or three short novels to read aloud from each week. I read the opening chapters and then stop at a cliff-hanger. As a result, students are so curious to find out what happens at the end that they'll seek out the book to finish during the summer. I also hand out a suggested reading list that includes the titles and authors of excellent books with summer themes.

DOLORES SEAMSTER

Passport To Summer Adventure

My name is_____

What I like most about summer is_____

_____

_____

My favorite summer sport is_____

My favorite summer food is_____

Instructions for Summer Adventurers

1. On the back of this paper, write what you would like to do this summer. Describe places you would like to visit. Also tell about people you would like to get to know.

2. Keep a summer journal or scrapbook. Record what you do and how you feel. Add drawings, photographs, ticket stubs, pressed flowers or leaves, and anything else you would like as a souvenir.

3. When you're stuck for something fun to do this summer, check out this checklist. Put a check next to each one you try.

Summer Activities Checklist
Fun for One

☐ Explore your neighborhood
☐ Read a book of magic tricks
☐ Perform magic tricks
☐ Make a card for Father's Day
☐ Bird watch
☐ Learn a song
☐ Write a song or a poem
☐ Go on a picnic
☐ Sell homemade lemonade
☐ Roller-skate
☐ Create an unusual sandwich
☐ Read a joke book
☐ Tell the jokes

☐ Begin a collection of anything
☐ Read a new book
☐ Visit a friend or relative
☐ Ride your bike
☐ Build a birdhouse
☐ Jog every morning
☐ Go to the movies
☐ Pretend you're a movie star
☐ Sketch a person or an animal
☐ Make up a new language
☐ Write a mystery story
☐ Paint a picture
☐ Write a letter

Thrills Galore for Two or More

☐ Create a new game and play it
☐ Hold a summer Olympics with the kids in the neighborhood
☐ Put on a play and perform it on July 4
☐ Play a board game
☐ Organize a science fair in your garage or back yard
☐ Make homemade instruments and have a concert for parents
☐ Start a club for readers, writers, bike riders, or another group
☐ Have a pet show
☐ Write and deliver a neighborhood newspaper
☐ Go anywhere in a group (try a museum, park, or the movies)